RED TAPE

Exordium

RED TAPE is everywhere and everywhere it is abhorred. How can any product of the human mind be so unpopular yet so widespread and so enduring? That is the mystery to which this book is addressed.

Lexicographers seem to agree that the term red tape derives from the ribbon once used to tie up legal documents in England. Because the common law gives great weight to precedent, every judicial decision must have been preceded by a thorough search of the records for guidance and authority. Such a system presumes that records of every transaction are punctiliously filed and cross-filed. We may surmise, therefore, that legions of clerks and lawyers spent a good deal of their time tying and untying the ribbon-bound folders.

Meanwhile, citizens and administrative officers trying to get action must have fretted and fumed while they waited for the meticulous minions to complete their patient unwrapping and rewrapping. And they must have exploded in outrage when, after all that, action was blocked on grounds of some obscure ancient decision or, still worse, because no unequivocal precedent could be found.

1

"Can we see where you keep the red tape?"

Hence the emergence of red tape as a despised symbol. The ribbon has long since disappeared, but the hated conditions and practices it represents continue, keeping the symbol alive. My purpose in examining them is to suggest an explanation of the incredible hardihood of those detested phenomena and thus to illuminate proposals for reform.

There isn't much serious literature on red tape, so I had to work largely from impressions formed in the course of three decades of studying public administration. I have drawn most heavily on administration in the federal government, but I believe the discussion has wider application—to other governments, at the very least, and to private organizations as well. No large organization seems to be immune to the symptoms of red tape.

The discussion consists of three parts. The first describes what is abhorred and why it is abhorred. The second explains how lofty motives and reasonable methods produce such abhorrent results. The third reviews strategies for improving things and the prospects for adoption of each of the strategies.

I have tried throughout the book to maintain clinical detachment from the subject. I don't find it revolting, infuriat-

2

RED TAPE

Its Origins, Uses, and Abuses

HERBERT KAUFMAN

THE BROOKINGS INSTITUTION

Washington, D.C.

The calligraphic images appearing in this book are taken from Johann Georg Schwandner, *Calligraphia Latina* (Vienna, 1756; Dover edition, 1958). They were drawn by Ferdinand von Freisleben and engraved by J. Kaspar Schwab. Schwandner (1716–91) was Librarian of the Imperial Library at Vienna.

The cartoons are reproduced with permission, as follows: Page 2, © 1976 Mobil Oil Corporation; page 17, GRIN AND BEAR IT by Lichty & Wagner, © Field Enterprises, Inc., 1976, reproduced courtesy Field Newspaper Syndicate; page 24, GRIN AND BEAR IT by Lichty & Wagner, © Field Enterprises, Inc., 1977, reproduced courtesy Field Newspaper Syndicate; page 55, reproduced courtesy *The Wall Street Journal* and Glenn Bernhardt; page 59, © 1976 Mobil Oil Corporation.

Library of Congress Cataloging in Publication Data:

Kaufman, Herbert, 1922–
   Red tape, its origins, uses, and abuses.

   Includes bibliographical references.
     1. United States—Executive departments—Management.
   2. United States—Politics and government. 3. Bureaucracy. 4. Public administration. I. Title.
JK421.K39   353   77-11083
ISBN 0-8157-4842-6
ISBN 0-8157-4841-8 pbk.

3 4 5 6 7 8 9

THE BROOKINGS INSTITUTION is an independent organization devoted to nonpartisan research, education, and publication in economics, government, foreign policy, and the social sciences generally. Its principal purposes are to aid in the development of sound public policies and to promote public understanding of issues of national importance.

The Institution was founded on December 8, 1927, to merge the activities of the Institute for Government Research, founded in 1916, the Institute of Economics, founded in 1922, and the Robert Brookings Graduate School of Economics and Government, founded in 1924.

The Board of Trustees is responsible for the general administration of the Institution, while the immediate direction of the policies, program, and staff is vested in the President, assisted by an advisory committee of the officers and staff. The by-laws of the Institution state: "It is the function of the Trustees to make possible the conduct of scientific research, and publication, under the most favorable conditions, and to safeguard the independence of the research staff in the pursuit of their studies and in the publication of the results of such studies. It is not a part of their function to determine, control, or influence the conduct of particular investigations or the conclusions reached."

The President bears final responsibility for the decision to publish a manuscript as a Brookings book. In reaching his judgment on the competence, accuracy, and objectivity of each study, the President is advised by the director of the appropriate research program and weighs the views of a panel of expert outside readers who report to him in confidence on the quality of the work. Publication of a work signifies that it is deemed a competent treatment worthy of public consideration but does not imply endorsement of conclusions or recommendations.

The Institution maintains its position of neutrality on issues of public policy in order to safeguard the intellectual freedom of the staff. Hence interpretations or conclusions in Brookings publications should be understood to be solely those of the authors and should not be attributed to the Institution, to its trustees, officers, or other staff members, or to the organizations that support its research.

Foreword

THIS BOOK was sired by the late Kermit Gordon. While President of the Brookings Institution, he remarked to Herbert Kaufman, senior fellow in the Governmental Studies program, that there was no serious book on government red tape. Satires, laments, denunciations, yes. But no analytical treatment of where red tape comes from and what can—and cannot—be done about it. Gordon thought the gap in the literature ought to be corrected. Thus was this little volume conceived.

There is no question that the manuscript would have been better had Gordon been able to bring his powerful intellect, wisdom, and great experience to bear on it. But he died before the first draft of the manuscript was completed. Nevertheless, his comments on the original outline and his preliminary discussions of the project with the author contributed greatly to the final product. A profound debt to him is gratefully acknowledged.

Kaufman was also given invaluable assistance by a number of readers who strove to save him from errors of approach and fact. Writing about red tape turned out to mean writing about the whole governmental process; keeping the subject in focus, and the parts of the analysis in proper balance, required candid advice from thoughtful, informed critics. He was well and generously served by the criticisms of James D. Farrell, Chester E. Finn, Jr., Hugh Heclo, Mark D. Littler, Richard P. Nathan, Paul Quirk, Herbert Roback, James L. Sundquist, and two additional readers whose great help is openly acknowledged even though their names, by custom, are withheld.

The book was edited by Elizabeth H. Cross. Radmila Nikolič magically turned illegible drafts into clean, readable copy.

The views expressed in his study are the author's and should not be attributed to the trustees, officers, or other staff members of the Brookings Institution.

BRUCE K. MACLAURY
President

Washington, D.C.
June 1977

Contents

ing, or funny. Mostly, I find it puzzling. I suspect, however, that I would have lost interest in it in a short while—there's a limit to the fascination of any puzzle—if it had not compelled me to speculate about the kind of organizational and political life we have fashioned for ourselves. Examined in that setting, red tape turns out to be at the core of our institutions rather than an excrescence on them. It is a sobering subject indeed.

Object of Loathing

ONCE in a long while, a voice is raised in defense of red tape. Or at least in explanation of it.[1] These voices are almost never heard. They are drowned in an unceasing chorus of denunciation. Everybody seems to hate red tape.

I say "seems to" because the apparent unanimity conceals significant differences. One person's "red tape" may be another's treasured safeguard. The term is applied to a bewildering variety of organizational practices and features.

Still, a common set of complaints is embedded in most definitions even though the complaints refer to different

1. For instance, Paul H. Appleby, *Big Democracy* (Knopf, 1945), chap. 6; Dwight Waldo, "Government by Procedure," in Fritz Morstein Marx, ed., *Elements of Public Administration* (Prentice-Hall, 1946); Charles S. Hyneman, *Bureaucracy in a Democracy* (Harper, 1950), chap. 24; Alvin W. Gouldner, "Red Tape as a Social Problem," in Robert K. Merton and others, eds., *Reader in Bureaucracy* (Free Press, 1952).

One common theme that runs through all of these essays is the relativity of red tape. Appleby: "Red tape is that part of my business you don't know anything about" (p. 64). Waldo: "One man's red tape is another man's system" (p. 399). Hyneman: "Red tape is a special term for a special dislike" (p. 522). Gouldner: "red tape as a social problem cannot be explained unless the frame of reference employed by the individual who uses this label is understood" (p. 411).

4

specific irritants. When people rail against red tape, they mean that they are subjected to too many constraints, that many of the constraints seem pointless, and that agencies seem to take forever to act. That is, we detest our *respective* forms of red tape, but for the same reasons.

TOO MANY CONSTRAINTS

We all hate to be told we have to do something or may not do something. Even if we actually enjoy the compulsory tasks and dislike the forbidden ones, the command rankles. The element of compulsion itself is distasteful. And it is much worse if we are forced to do what we don't want to do, and are prohibited from doing what we strongly want to do.

Today, you can hardly turn around without bumping into some federal restraint or requirement. It wasn't always so; there was a time you could embark on almost any venture without encountering a single federal constraint. Now, however, if you should take it into your head, say, to manufacture and market a new product, you would probably run into statutes and administrative regulations on labor relations, occupational safety, product safety, and air purity. Your advertising would probably fall within the jurisdiction of the Federal Trade Commission. The Department of Justice would be interested in your relations with your competitors. Should you want to raise capital by the sale of stock or bonds, you would fall under the Securities and Exchange Commission. You would need export licenses from the Department of Commerce to sell your product in some areas of the world. Federal prohibitions against race, age, and sex discrimination in hiring and promotion would apply to you. If you were to extend credit to your customers, you might fall under truth-in-lending laws. You would have to file sundry reports for tax, social security, pension, and census purposes. In some fields—communication, transportation, energy, insurance, and banking, for instance—restrictions and oversight are especially stringent. But firms of all kinds, large and small, are subject to diverse federal requirements. You can't just start and run a business without reference to federal specifications and officials.

Business is not the only activity affected this way. Labor unions, foundations, political parties, universities, lobbyists, and even farmers are similarly constrained. Every recipient of government subsidies, loans, and other forms of public assistance finds these benefits come with conditions and obligations that have to be satisfied. The government's reach is very long.

The sheer mass of binding official promulgations and interventions in the marketplace begins to be oppressive. The number seems to increase steadily. The media revel in embarrassing exposés. Although it is possible that this impression is engendered partly by the irritations of corresponding actions by state and local governments and the private sector of society, which are no less prolific,[2] the federal government, being the largest and most visible institution, attracts a disproportionate share of the venom. Many people seem to feel it is closing in on them from all sides, and it is to this sensation that they react when they excoriate red tape.

They are dismayed also because the torrent of requirements descending on them is too overwhelming for them to comply with. Conscientious, upright citizens are often distressed when they find themselves in violation of government directives, yet they simply cannot keep up with the flood. Said one desperate victim, "We have reached the saturation level, and each new law and each new agency at every level of government . . . is forcing decent citizens into involuntary noncompliance with the law. Now, this is tragic when upstanding honest citizens just can't comply with the laws."[3]

2. *Government Reports and Statistics*, S. Rept. 1616, 90:2 (Government Printing Office, 1968). On p. 37, the Senate Select Committee on Small Business concludes, "As for State and local government reporting, we can no longer close our eyes to the fact that it has become equally burdensome with the Federal system."

3. *The Federal Paperwork Burden*, S. Rept. 93-125, 93:1 (GPO, 1973), p. 55.

It is certainly undeniable that the output of the federal government is prodigious. Congress alone produces over a thousand printed pages of public laws in an average session. Federal courts routinely publish thousands of pages of decisions and opinions every year. The regulations of federal administrative agencies, including both draft and final forms, total more than 50,000 printed pages annually. One especially prolific agency was said to have issued enough documents to make a stack seventeen feet high.[4] Of course, there is substantial redundancy in this outpouring. Moreover, only a small percentage of it is likely to affect any given individual or organization. Still, it is easy to understand why red tape has become a matter for concern. The stream appears to be at flood stage and relentlessly rising.

Another indicator of its ostensible menace is the volume of material the federal government requires people to submit to it: the total number of submissions has been put at more than 2 billion a year, or nearly ten for each man, woman, and child in the country. Over 70 percent of these, it is true, are connected with taxes, chiefly for internal revenue and social security, but this means the impact is extremely broad. Moreover, the remaining 600 million are highly diversified; indeed, the number of different forms authorized for distribution to the public by federal agencies exceeds five thousand.[5]

Many people are hard hit by these requirements. A "Mom and Pop" store with a gross annual income of less than $30,000 had to file tax forms fifty-two times a year. A firm with fewer than fifty employees had to prepare seventy-five or eighty submissions a year for various agencies.[6] A small securities broker-dealer sent thirty-eight submissions to seven different agencies in one year.[7] A plant employing seventy-five people had two of them working half time solely to draw up

4. Ibid., p. 4.
5. Ibid., p. 2; *The Federal Paperwork Jungle*, H. Rept. 52, 89:1 (GPO, 1965), pp. 23 ff.
6. *The Federal Paperwork Burden*, S. Rept. 93-125, pp. 8, 2.
7. *The Federal Paperwork Burden*, Hearings before the Senate Subcommittee on Government Regulation of the Select Committee on Small Business, 92:2 (GPO, 1972), pt. 4, p. 1430.

compulsory plans and reports; a company with a hundred employees made seventy filings or payments each year to the Internal Revenue Service alone; a small radio station assigned two employees full time for four months to supply all the information specified by the Federal Communications Commission for license renewal, and another reported that its application for renewal weighed forty-five pounds.[8] The chairman of the board of a large pharmaceutical firm claimed that his company prepared 27,000 government forms or reports a year at a cost of $5 million. ("We spend," he added, "more man-hours filling out government forms or reports than we do on research for cancer and heart disease combined.")[9] Even personal income tax forms, despite great progress in simplifying them, are now complicated enough to require a good deal of effort by most taxpayers and to have fostered numerous commercial services that help them with the tasks of computation and filing.

Nobody escapes. Each of us has his or her own complaint. Each hears similar complaints from others. Each realizes that his or her discontent, though it represents only an infinitesimal segment of the broad band of government activities, is part of a pattern too vast for one person to perceive. No wonder everybody begins to feel suffocated by red tape. The sheer magnitude of the government's demands and constraints, no matter how reasonable each of them is individually, guarantees this reaction.

"POINTLESS" CONSTRAINTS

From the point of view of the individual citizen, however, they are *not* all reasonable. Some of them make no sense to the people who must comply with them. If people find self-evidently justified requirements intolerable when they be-

8. *The Federal Paperwork Burden*, S. Rept. 93-125, pp. 4, 5, 10.
9. Richard D. Wood, "Paperwork, Paperwork," *Washington Post*, July 12, 1976.

come too numerous, imagine how they feel about requirements that seem pointless. It would not take many of these
to discredit the whole body of government constraints.

Of course, what is pointless to one person may seem essential to another. Values and perspectives vary. Also, the
reasons for any given program or policy may be persuasive,
though not obvious; inadequate explanation may account for
its ostensible pointlessness, or perhaps some critics fail to
evaluate it carefully. Pointlessness is relative.

But it is people's *perceptions* of government constraints,
not objective measures of reasonableness, that lead them to
attack some constraints as red tape. With torrents of new
promulgations pouring from government organs, if even a
small proportion strike some people as senseless, the absolute
number of the disaffected must be large. From all indications,
that is exactly what happens.

"Irrelevant" Requirements

For example, many complaints about red tape come from
critics who believe that they have been compelled to obey
commands that should not apply to them and probably were
never meant to. Thus the legislative counsel of the National
Society of Public Accountants, testifying about some reports
collected from businessmen by the Census Bureau, told a
Senate subcommittee:

The detailed complexity of some of the census economic forms has
questionable value. . . . The compilation of a great mass of statistics
has little value to the persons whom it was apparently meant to
benefit. . . .
Information, I must add, that in large part was supplied by the
people who basically do not need it. In my own practice—and in
this I am experienced—I know of no business that uses any of the
census statistics in any way, even though they must supply this
information.[10]

Similarly, a small retailer stormed:

I have here a 32-page booklet, published by the Department of
Labor, explaining what we must do to comply with the recent

10. *The Federal Paperwork Burden*, Hearings, pt. 5, pp. 1953-54.

9

Occupational Safety and Health Act. It also contains copies of three new records we employers must maintain and then keep on hand for two years. I must sit down with these materials and figure out what I have to do to comply with this law, and then see to it that the requirements are carried out. Yet retailing isn't even a target industry of OSHA.[11]

To which a small New Hampshire manufacturer added:

OSHA was written for companies like Ford Motors which actually owns a huge hospital in Dearborn. The act was not written for my little company with a medicine cabinet containing a bottle of Mercurochrome and a bottle of aspirin.[12]

Testimony of this kind from a number of witnesses persuaded the Senate Select Committee on Small Business that

the Federal bureaucracy, the governmental units most removed from the people, fails to understand the circumstances or the need of the private citizens or the small business. . . . Bureaucrats, accustomed to dealing with situations of massive scale, find it virtually impossible to comprehend the stress their demands . . . place on the small firm.[13]

The problem of irrelevant requirements was said to be so pervasive as to arouse suspicions of a conspiracy:

Some small businessmen who make little or no use of officially compiled information, themselves, suspect that there exists an unholy alliance between Government and big business in these matters and that the information supplied by them to the Government is often used by market researchers, location specialists, and sales analysts of the large companies to the detriment of small business.[14]

But it is not only small businessmen who object. The representative of the pharmaceutical manufacturer mentioned earlier observed,

Our application to the FDA for a drug for treatment of arthritis consisted of 120,000 pages. . . . About 25 percent of these pages—or 30,000 of them—contained information that was important to the evaluation of the drug by FDA. The other 90,000 pages contained incredibly detailed records.[15]

Officials themselves concede the prevalence of wide disparities in viewpoint between themselves and the public. A

11. *The Federal Paperwork Burden*, S. Rept. 93-125, p. 54.
12. *The Federal Paperwork Burden*, Hearings, pt. 6, p. 2178.
13. *The Federal Paperwork Burden*, S. Rept. 93-125, p. 3.
14. *Government Reports and Statistics*, S. Rept. 1616, p. 2.
15. Wood, "Paperwork, Paperwork."

group of high-level Washington administrators ("admirals and generals of the bureaucracy," they were called by a commentator) were brought to New York City to learn at first hand something about the life of the poor. Many of them were astonished. "Here we are in Washington passing on licenses for Con Ed," one of them said, "and we never think about how people like this are on the other end of the line." "We are too insulated in Washington," another remarked. "We don't realize what's going on out there in the country."[16]

"Out there in the country," countless Americans agree with them and disparage as useless and irrelevant many of the things the federal government requires and forbids.

Duplicative and Contradictory Requirements

Even when they acknowledge the usefulness and relevance of specific requirements and prohibitions, people are incensed at having to do the same thing many times for different agencies when it appears to them that once would be enough if the government were more efficient. Witnesses testifying at congressional hearings complained of this again and again. One observed,

In the requirement of the reporting and process of compliance with the Equal Employment Opportunity requirements under the law . . . it seems to us that if we work for five or six agencies of the Government we should only have to . . . indicate that we are in compliance with the law one time. But by reason of the fact that the bureaucrats . . . in each agency want exactly the same thing, instead of filing once . . . we have to file as many different sets of these as we work for different agencies.[17]

Another explained,

We are not unreasonable people in business. We realize that you have to have a record and you have to measure accomplishments and all of these things, but we do not believe that it takes the same record 10 different times to produce the results that are actually required by law.[18]

The congressional committee joined in wondering "why

16. Edith Evans Asbury, *New York Times*, October 16, 1975.
17. *The Federal Paperwork Burden*, S. Rept. 93-125, pp. 12–13.
18. Ibid., p. 15.

he must report similar information to several Federal agencies, and identical information to a federal and to a state agency," and concluded:

The form-maker, sitting in Washington surrounded by hundreds of other bureaucrats, does not comprehend the urgency of this man's point of view, the man is only being asked to spend a few hours filling out a form. What the bureaucrat fails to understand is that the few hours his agency requires multiplied by the requests of several other Federal agencies places an enormous strain on the resources of the small enterprise.[19]

Executing the same forms over and over is not only boring and, to the people who must complete them, a foolish result of poor management; it adds to expenses. Nobody knows exactly how general such duplication is, but the scale of government operations is so large that it apparently occurs frequently and casts a shadow on the need for most of the things the government does or demands.

Still more irritating from the point of view of the conscientiously law-abiding person, in government as well as in private life, are government requirements drawn in such a way that to obey one seems to lead to violations of the other. I say "seems to" advisedly. The apparent inconsistencies are often ambiguities rather than contradictions. But even ambiguities impose dilemmas and burdens on those who strive to comply; each individual must resolve for himself or herself uncertainties created by poor draftsmanship, inadvertent contradictions, or deliberate avoidance of hard choices on the part of officials, and the most painstaking attempt to obey all provisions of all applicable sets of requirements meticulously may eventually be judged to have violated one or another.

For example, legislation protecting the right to privacy may conflict with the spirit, if not the letter, of the Freedom of Information Act. To take another case, one strategy for reducing racial discrimination is to prohibit inquiries about

19. Ibid., pp. 15, 4.

race on application forms of all kinds in both the private sector and in government, but another strategy is to require records on the treatment of minority applicants so that patterns of prejudice may be exposed and reversed; people can get caught between the two. A third illustration is the uncertain line between the expectation that career public servants will carry out the edicts of their political superiors without regard to their own predilections and the principle that duty requires them to disobey improper orders. These conflicting guidelines shift the difficulties of reconciliation from the promulgators of official policy to the individual private citizen or public employee without much guidance and with the possibility of punishment no matter what course is chosen.

Duplications and contradictions cannot be blamed entirely on the large number of national laws and agencies. The federal system, just because it has three levels of government, would produce such frictions even if each level issued few documents. Shoddy legislative draftsmanship and poor administration, which can appear even in small governments, would also make difficulties. But there can be little doubt that the scale of operations of the federal government contributes heavily to the problem. Officers and employees in a vast system find it impossible to keep track of all the actions taken in earlier times or in other parts of the governmental structure. Furthermore, in a highly fragmented and fluid administrative community, few officials feel bound by the policies of their predecessors and colleagues. Consistency and tidiness are hard to preserve in a far-flung, complex environment.

Inertia

Once requirements and practices are instituted, they tend to remain in force long after the conditions that spawned them have disappeared. A committee of the House of Representatives, reporting on federal paperwork requirements in

13

1965, commented on "obsolete and archaistic reports" and offered two illustrations. One was

the Bureau of Customs forms for the entry and clearance of vessels at U.S. ports. As brought out in the subcommittee hearings, these forms have not changed to any great extent since 1790, and merchant vessels today are required to report on the number of guns mounted.[20]

The other was also a maritime example—the shipping articles that merchant seamen were required to sign before voyages, based on legislation of 1872 and 1873.[21] Among the articles was a Sunday food schedule as out of date as kerosene lanterns and buggy whips. All the same, the empty provisions were still solemnized a century later.

Similarly, a single embarrassing incident may inspire practices that go on and on at great cost and minimal benefit. As a former director of the Bureau of the Budget put it,

The public servant soon learns that successes rarely rate a headline, but governmental blunders are front page news. This recognition encourages the development of procedures designed less to achieve successes than to avoid blunders. Let it be discovered that the Army is buying widgets from private suppliers while the Navy is disposing of excess widgets at a lower price; the reporter will win a Pulitzer prize and the Army and Navy will establish procedures for liaison, review, and clearance which will prevent a recurrence and which will also introduce new delays and higher costs into the process of buying or selling anything. It may cost a hundred times more to prevent the occurrence of occasional widget episodes, but no one will complain.[22]

Presumably, federal administration is shot through with cases of this kind, though nobody can be sure. Nor, of course, can anybody certify that continuous review of government operations to get rid of such ludicrous requirements would not cost more than letting them remain on the books. The search for outmoded practices takes government time and money, yet old, unchanging procedures, once learned, are

20. *The Federal Paperwork Jungle,* H. Rept. 52, pp. 30–31.
21. Ibid.
22. Kermit Gordon, "After Vietnam: Domestic Issues and Public Policies" (speech delivered to the Stanford Business Conference, San Francisco, February 19, 1969; processed).

easily followed, and utterly obsolete ones are usually ignored by everyone. So the burden of correcting them may be greater than that of letting them linger. Whether or not the direct cost of eliminating them exceeds the direct cost of enduring them, however, there is no doubt that even occasional exposures of such anomalies bring discredit on the whole establishment. And when enough requirements are on the books, as in the federal government, elimination of these embarrassments is a virtual impossibility.

Programs That Fail

Nothing, however, is as likely to render requirements pointless, in the opinion of some of those who must comply with them and of neutral observers, as constraints that obviously do not produce the results proclaimed as justifications for them. Restrictions and burdens imposed for announced ends that are never attained are probably the hardest to bear.

Government regulation of business illustrates the point. Many regulatory programs originated in response to demands for government suppression of abuses, either actual or potential. The prices of products or services were seen as excessively high, the quality unfairly or dangerously low, the supply uncertain. Consumers of these goods and services, denied what they wanted in the marketplace, asked the government to intervene to prevent these deficiencies. Such intervention was accomplished by new legislation, new agencies, new regulations and orders and controls. These measures were deemed by their backers to be worth their cost because they would eliminate or reduce evils. Naturally, if the evils did not disappear, or if even worse evils took their place, the regulatory programs would make no sense.

Gradually, some observers began to suspect that the programs were falling far short of their proclaimed objectives, or even making things worse. In the first place, the observers noticed that the regulated interests often benefited more from regulation than consumers did. The interests were relieved of competition, yet the controls on them allegedly did not shore up quality or hold down prices in return for this security. In a free market, low-quality or overpriced practitioners or manufacturers, shorn of official protection, would presumably be forced to improve quality, lower prices, or go out of business. Regulation has therefore been given low grades by critics from all sectors of the political spectrum.[23]

In the second place, it has been said that regulatory officials acquire the same perspectives and values as the interests they regulate.[24] The two groups are in constant contact and thus become indistinguishable, especially since personnel move from one to the other freely. In any event, in the contest to exert influence on the regulators, consumers are ordinarily outclassed by the well-organized, well-heeled, well-informed, well-connected, continuously functioning, experienced producers. Furthermore, the incentive structure motivates the powerful more effectively than the weak; a regulatory decision meaning millions to a firm often costs individual consumers less than the cost of protesting it, so it would be irrational for individual consumers to fight even though the loss hurts them deeply. Adding to dissatisfaction is the ability of regulated interests to pass along to consumers their costs of exerting pressure and of fighting consumer suits. Under these conditions, ask the critics, how effective can regulation be?

Measures to nullify these biases have been adopted in many jurisdictions. These include limited bans on employment of regulatory staff by regulated industries, insulation of decisionmakers from pressure, and authorization of class-action

23. See, for example, Edward F. Cox, Robert C. Fellmeth, and John E. Schulz, *"The Nader Report" on the Federal Trade Commission* (Baron, 1969); Louis M. Kohlmeier, Jr., *The Regulators* (Harper and Row, 1969).

24. Roger G. Noll, *Reforming Regulation: An Evaluation of the Ash Council Proposals* (Brookings Institution, 1971), chap. 3, especially p. 31: "The preceding discussion of regulatory failures only summarizes a vast literature in which regulators are accused of being excessively concerned about the welfare of the regulated." See also the item on extensive interchange of personnel between regulatory agencies and regulated industries by David Burnham, *New York Times*, January 2, 1976.

*"Gentlemen, the bad news is the company is in
a state of bankruptcy.... The good news is we
have complied with federal rules and regulations."*

suits. Nevertheless, complaints about the regulatory process
continue, and some commentators have characterized it as
largely symbolic, adopted for the purpose of quieting public
discontent by a show of governmental action when those who
adopt it know that the programs will be vitiated in practice.[25]

Indeed, regulatory bodies have even been called agents of

25. Murray Edelman, *The Symbolic Uses of Politics* (University of
Illinois Press, 1967).

the regulated rather than their masters. That is why regulated interests, once the bitterest foes of regulation, are now among the most ardent defenders of their regulatory agencies, and why some industries have actively sought to be placed under regulation. By the same token, consumer organizations are among the most vehement critics, claiming that consumers, the ostensible beneficiaries, have been victimized. Those who subscribe to this interpretation of regulation regard as pointless all the laws, regulations, hearings, procedural complications, administrative machinery, and other trappings of government control and oversight of business. In their eyes, the programs are failures, and the constraints associated with them are so much useless red tape.

Other constraints are derided as pointless not so much because they are turned to the advantage of the people they were supposed to restrain as because they are not one hundred percent effective. Take the procedures, described later, to ensure the integrity of government funds, the impartiality of the civil service, and the fairness of government contracting. These impose burdens, inconveniences, and costs within the government and on all who deal with it. Yet scandals occur repeatedly. Not a year goes by without exposés of public officers and employees being deceived or bribed by unscrupulous citizens or taking advantage of their positions to enrich themselves. Political connections reputedly do no harm when one is trying to get ahead in government service. High officials have been lavishly entertained by major defense contractors. Corruption and favoritism persist despite layers of requirements, platoons of overseers, and convolutions of procedures intended to prevent them.[26]

Of course, one might infer from the exposure and prosecution of such infractions that the system is working. But if you are incommoded by preventive measures that are repeatedly violated, you are more likely to see the measures as useless. When violators are able to penetrate the defenses yet honest

26. See chapter 2, notes 63 and 64, below.

people who would never think of defrauding the government or abusing their authority must go through all the rigamarole set up to thwart scoundrels, it is understandable that the honest people grow resentful. They would doubtless concede that some would-be violators are deterred by the safeguards. But to make large numbers suffer in order to reduce the percentage of noncompliance by a tiny fraction does not seem rational. "It usually doesn't pay," said one congressional witness, "to set up a system—any system—to make two percent of a group 'behave' at the expense of the other 98 percent."[27] Moreover, insult is added to injury; it appears to some observers that "the Government has a deep and abiding distrust of citizens generally" and "assumes every citizen is automatically a crook."[28] To people with this outlook, catching the handful of crooks does not prove that all the troublesome constraints designed to avert dishonesty justify all the machinery; rather, it proves that the machinery is not worth the hardships it inflicts on the innocent.

This skeptical view is not universally shared, but it has many adherents. And those who subscribe to it perceive government requirements in general as red tape. Government controls are seen not only as failing to work, but as inherently incapable of working. In this view, therefore, they are neither justified nor justifiable.

QUAGMIRE

Even programs considered successful in the long run, however, will be called red tape if they are also considered excessively slow in acting on pending matters. Such perceptions are relative, of course; people waiting for desperately needed financial assistance, for contracts that make the difference between profit and loss, or for licenses without which they

27. *The Federal Paperwork Burden,* S. Rept. 93-125, p. 11.
28. Ibid., p. 12.

may not do business are apt to believe that operations are much slower than uninvolved observers believe them to be, and certainly much slower than public servants toiling furiously against budgetary limitations and procedural constraints believe them to be. But large numbers of people are victims at one time or another of delays when they are impatient for action. Often, this being one of their few direct contacts with the government, they conclude that the whole system is bogged down.

Indeed, there are *always* people waiting for government action of some kind. Except in matters of law enforcement, government agencies ordinarily respond to applications and demands on them—and even in many law-enforcement cases, act on the complaint of an interested party. Individuals and organizations petition them for all sorts of things: licenses and permits, welfare benefits, subsidies, tax refunds, payments for goods or services rendered, pension benefits, insurance benefits, veterans' benefits, loans, and others. They also seek changes in standing rules and regulations, in procedures, and even in the location of field offices. Millions of decisions of these kinds are made routinely every day and apparently, despite the impatience of the petitioners, are made promptly enough to keep most people quiet, if not happy. Some, however, do become mired.

For example, it is not extraordinary for federal agencies to take two years to reach decisions. In one state, officials decided to forgo federal funds for an urgently needed highway because the two or three years required to get them meant that construction costs would meanwhile have increased more than the amount of the aid.[29] And extreme delays go far beyond this; the Food and Drug Administration took a decade to develop standards of identity for peanut butter,[30] and the Federal Communications Commission was warned by a fed-

29. James Feron, *New York Times*, October 27, 1975.
30. William F. Pedersen, Jr., "Formal Records and Informal Rulemaking," *Yale Law Journal*, vol. 85 (November 1975), p. 44.

eral court to pick up the pace of its proceedings after a case instituted ten years earlier came before the bench.[31] Some construction industry spokesmen charged that more than a decade often elapsed between the initial studies of a federal project and project authorization, and another five to ten years before project completion.[32] Extenuating circumstances account for these snail-paced proceedings, but explanations seldom overcome the negative image the delays engender. Explanations or no explanations, ten years are deemed too many by most observers; that to them is red tape under any circumstances.

Horror stories add to the negative impact. A United States congressman, for instance, publicly recorded one of those depressing tales that tarnish the reputation of the whole governmental process. A workingman was afflicted with severe mental illness and committed to a mental hospital. His parents, whom he helped support, applied for and received his disability benefits, part of which went to the hospital for his maintenance. After a while, he improved enough to win off-grounds parole, and he took a menial job. His parents, as required by law, notified the Social Security Administration, which promptly terminated the disability benefits (even though a nine-month trial period of continued benefits, to see if the insured really had overcome his handicap, would have been permissible under the law).

The young man proved unequal to the stress and returned to the hospital. His parents applied for reinstatement of benefits, but their application was denied, apparently in part because they were unable to get a supporting letter from the hospital physician, who feared it might be the basis of a suit against him. They filed an appeal. Nothing happened. According to them, they made repeated inquiries about the status of the appeal. Still nothing happened. The adverse

31. Kenneth Culp Davis, *Administrative Law of the Seventies, Supplementing Administrative Law Treatise* (Lawyers Cooperative Publishing, 1976), p. 282.
32. *The Federal Paperwork Burden*, S. Rept. 93-125, p. 14.

initial decision left them unhappy, but at least they could take some action to have it reversed or modified; the delay on the appeal left them without benefits or formal recourse, an utterly frustrating position.

They therefore turned to the congressman for help, and in the spring of 1975 he assigned one of his caseworkers to assist them and wrote personally to the Commissioner of Social Security. By the time October rolled around, the worker was still in the hospital, his parents were still without his disability benefits, and there was still no ruling on the appeal. "As of this date," the congressman fumed, "he still has not received a decision on his case: 1 year and 188 days after his case was opened." Nor was that all:

As of this date, my constituent has not received his hearing or notification of his hearing date. We do know that depending on whom one speaks to in the Social Security system, he has the same purported file in three different places, none of which can be produced on request. Note, too, that each person in each [part of the] agency attempted to be helpful, but also claimed no knowledge or responsibility for action or lack of action in this case. As I recount this, I find myself angry, not only at the miscarriage of justice . . . but also because the system is so elaborate and so impervious to direct human appeal that responsibility can be placed on no one person's shoulder.

Personally, I think that the Social Security Administration has treated Mr. S. and his parents with the consideration that one would expect of George Orwell's Big Brother in his novel, "1984," and the rationality of the grand inquisitor in Kafka's "The Trial."[33]

Even if the hyperbole is discounted, it was clearly a lamentable affair. And when it moved a U.S. congressman to air the situation in testimony before a congressional committee and in a major newspaper, it contributed to a hostile, scornful attitude toward government requirements on the part of a good many people. A few such cases from time to time can reinforce and spread the attitude. The belief that government is a quagmire of red tape is thus diffused throughout the society notwithstanding the possible unrepresentativeness of the individual cases underlying it.

33. H. John Heinz III, *Washington Post*, October 14, 1975.

THE SCAPEGOATS

One reaction to the disagreeable consequences of profuse government requirements and prohibitions is to blame the profusion on the perniciousness or stupidity or laziness of government personnel. After all, the victims of red tape would not inflict such injuries and indignities on themselves, would they? Therefore the officers and employees who promulgate the laws and regulations must be responsible.

The accusations have enough surface plausibility to persuade some disgruntled citizens of their validity. It is conceivable that officials intent on aggrandizing their own power and protecting their own jobs would, unconsciously if not deliberately, contrive a blizzard of incomprehensible paper, a procedural maze, and a mass of technicalities that only someone completely familiar with these provisions could hope to find his way through. Then, insiders could not be easily replaced, even after changes in political leadership. Their decisions could be challenged by outsiders only with difficulty, for full-time specialists are not easily defeated by victims or insurgents who make their living at other pursuits and cannot devote themselves exclusively to operating the system. Even nominal superiors would have to bow to the experts in the structures the experts themselves created. It would be a clever, self-serving strategy for officials to spin out complicated webs of red tape, conferring on themselves a near-monopoly from which they could not be dislodged.

Conversely, it is equally plausible that official stupidity and laziness might be responsible for the crazy quilt of provisions and procedures in government. Dull, slothful public servants would have to be furnished with specific, minutely detailed rules for every conceivable situation because, lacking intelligence or initiative, they could not be trusted to devise sensible responses on their own. They would be likely to formulate unsuitable and pointless rules and decisions

*"Frankly, trimming the bureaucracy has me worried. . . .
It just means fewer people to handle all that red tape."*

either because they lacked the understanding to recognize irrelevancy and inappropriateness or because they were not industrious enough to check all the facts or trace all the effects of what they do. They would cling to familiar courses of action long after those methods ceased to be apposite. Wanting in the wisdom to invent responses quickly or adhering slavishly to established procedures and rote recitation of published regulations (the most imaginative behavior of which

24

such people would be capable and certainly the safest), they would take forever to arrive at solutions to problems.

Obviously, the two portrayals of officialdom are mutually contradictory. Nobody can be both diabolically clever and dull-witted at the same time, nor can those who invent and execute complicated strategies also be too indolent to put themselves out on any account. One might contend that some public servants are of one kind and some of the other, and that together they are responsible for all the red tape in government. But it is as hard to swallow the notion that knaves and fools are the dominant elements among thousands of government officers and employees as it would be to acquiesce in the suggestion that the whole population consists of only these two categories. There is no a priori reason to assume they are intellectually or morally inferior to the rest of us; the level of their mental gifts and their characters is by no means below that of the general populace.[34] Neither the conspiracy theory nor the incompetence theory seems to me a persuasive explanation for the abundance of government requirements and prohibitions or for the unhappy and unwanted effects of these constraints.

Indeed, government personnel are greatly disserved by red tape. They would like to get on with their missions as they see them, to pursue their program goals energetically, efficiently, speedily. They chafe at the obstacles placed in their way, the restraints imposed on them, the boundaries they must observe, the procedures they must follow. Nobody is more critical of red tape than they. To them, it is ironic that they should be blamed for it.

Unquestionably, they are tightly constrained. Their discretion is legally limited by statutes, regulations of sister agencies, judicial decisions, executive orders, and departmental directives. It is also politically limited by the need to accommodate powerful political figures and influential inter-

34. W. Lloyd Warner and others, *The American Federal Executive* (Yale University Press, 1963).

est groups, by the practical independence of nominal subordinates, by the demands of clienteles, and by the risks of adverse publicity in the communications media. So they are often prevented from moving forcefully and promptly when they would like to and compelled to yield to pressures when they would prefer to stand firm, even though this may mean an injustice is done or suffering is not relieved. They are also forced to allocate precious time and money to the endless demands for reports and information made by Congress and the public and other agencies, and to process vast streams of reports they don't want but are obliged by law to collect for the use of others.[35] In short, the costs, inconveniences, and burdens of government constraints oppress government workers as much as anybody.

In fact, perhaps more. Understandably, they see themselves as experts in their fields, yet many of the constraints on them are the work of people they regard as uninformed amateurs. Career diplomats who must answer to legislators with no experience in foreign affairs, urban specialists who must defer to interests from back-country farm regions, and professional military officers challenged at every turn by civilians with slight knowledge of military strategy and tactics, for example, grind their teeth in frustration. If people outside government think *they* are victims of irrelevant obligations and prohibitions, they should see what those *inside* have to put up with—at all levels, too.

35. For example, the Federal Aviation Administration listed 1,665 reports in its inventory of recurring reports in 1970; FAA Order 1340.3F, "Catalog of Approved FAA Recurring Reports—June, 1970," July 31, 1970. Of these, 215 were required by more than three dozen external bodies, including Congress, the White House, other departments and agencies, states, and various employee organizations. But many of the internal documents were also generated by external requests, such as reports on equal employment opportunity and employee safety. From the point of view of many officers of the FAA, all these obligations are merely distractions from their main jobs and lower the volume of end product per employee and per dollar of expenditure.

Note also some of the procedures for protecting representativeness in the government, described in chapter 2.

In lower echelons, subordinates are obliged to observe laws and regulations even when they think the contents are ill conceived. If they believe the contents are illegal or immoral and they are unable to persuade their superiors to make appropriate changes, they are expected to resign and protest from the outside; if they continue in service, they are supposed to obey (though, of course, some do stay and resist from within).[36] Resignation is not always a live option for everyone; many therefore stay on and try to comply with requirements they object to, hoping for better times eventually, when new leaders arrive. Meanwhile, they bemoan red tape.

Leaders are equally frustrated. Political superiors find administrative agencies less responsive to them than they would like because the agencies are bound by generations of accumulated obligations and restraints. Leaders therefore cannot do as much as they would like to shape administrative action to the image of their own philosophies or to the demands of their allies and constituents. They are also angry and embarrassed by their apparent inability to eliminate the red tape that everyone complains about; the persistence of red tape makes them seem unresponsive or powerless. Unable to get their own way or to do favors for their friends whenever they want, the highest government officials are frequently as enraged by the vast corpus of constraints embodied in official documents as any of their subordinates and as any private citizen. They are among the loudest and most intense critics.[37]

Public officers and employees get the blame for red tape, I suppose because they are the ones who personify the governmental action and inaction we all resent. Or maybe we blame them because we can't think of another plausible ex-

36. Albert O. Hirschman, *Exit, Voice, and Loyalty* (Harvard University Press, 1970).

37. Arthur M. Schlesinger, Jr., *A Thousand Days* (Houghton Mifflin, 1965), pp. 680–86; Richard P. Nathan, *The Plot That Failed* (Wiley, 1975), pp. 82–84; Stephen Hess, *Organizing the Presidency* (Brookings Institution, 1976), p. 9.

planation for the prevalence of something everybody pro-
fesses to loathe. It would not surprise me, however, if they are
merely scapegoats in a literal sense—bearers of the blame for
others. We may accuse them because, intuitively, we want to
divert the guilt from the real cause: ourselves. No one element of the population is responsible for all red tape or even
for most of it. In the next chapter, I shall try to show that we
all have a hand in it.

Of Our Own Making

Little drops of water,
Little grains of sand,
Make a mighty ocean
And a mighty land.

—NURSERY RHYME

IN SUGGESTING that responsibility for the massive outpouring of government requirements and restraints decried as red
tape is widely shared, I do not mean to imply that we manufacture red tape deliberately. For the most part, we do so
without realizing it. That we do so inadvertently, however,
does not alter the facts about the origins of the outpouring.
All of us together produce it.

Every restraint and requirement originates in somebody's
demand for it. Of course, each person does not will them all;
on the contrary, even the most broadly based interest groups
are concerned with only a relatively small band of the full
spectrum of government activities, and most interest groups
are narrowly specialized rather than broadly based. So each
constraint is the product of a fairly small number of claim-
ants. But there are so many of us, and such a diversity of interests among us, that modest individual demands result in

great stacks of official paper and bewildering procedural mazes.

Let me illustrate this contention by reviewing the effects of just two properties we have tried to infuse into our government: compassion and representativeness. Each of these is a cluster of attributes, not a single simple trait. And they are only two such clusters among many. But they account for a storm of complaints about red tape.

HOW COMPASSION SPAWNS RED TAPE

If the government were not driven to protect us from injury, for example, there would be many fewer governmental constraints and complicated procedures in our society. I exclude "common crimes" and the administration of criminal justice from this discussion—not because they are conceptually or practically distinct from other kinds of official prohibitions and obligations, but because, for obscure reasons, they are not usually regarded as red tape,[1] and because, in any event, they fall chiefly within the jurisdiction of the states rather than the federal government. The remaining protections are still vast, for the federal government tries in so many ways to prevent harm from befalling us.

Protecting People from Each Other

Take the relations between buyers and sellers. For a long time, these were left largely to negotiations between the parties to each transaction; the government had little to do with them. They were not *entirely* unregulated by public authority, the courts being available to parties aggrieved by deception or other injury. For the most part, though, remedies could be sought only after damages had been inflicted or at least only when damages were imminent. Hence the

1. Alvin W. Gouldner, "Red Tape as a Social Problem," in Robert K. Merton and others, eds., *Reader in Bureaucracy* (Free Press, 1952), p. 411.

warning that it was up to the buyer to beware. The government took no responsibility for the buyer's well-being.

Today, the government is deeply involved in trying to prevent injuries *before* they occur. People demanded its protection for many reasons—the marketplace worked too imperfectly to shield them from harm by venal or careless producers and distributors, the courts were uneconomic instruments of redress for individuals whose damages were of small monetary value, the amount of technical knowledge required to choose sensibly among the innumerable products offered for sale came to exceed what most of us could master, agreements between buyers and sellers began to impinge more and more heavily on persons not party to the negotiations or to the bargains struck, and social values changed as industrial society proved fertile soil for new philosophies. In response to the demands for governmental intervention provoked by these developments, the government interceded in more and more buyer-seller relations.

It has attempted, for instance, to assure the purity of food and the safety of drugs.[2] It has attempted to prevent false and misleading advertising.[3] It has attempted to reduce dangers from hazardous substances and products of all kinds.[4] It has attempted to improve the safety of passengers in public and private transportation.[5] These are just a few of the programs to raise the minimum standards of selected goods and services. Buyers still have to beware; the public programs fall short of absolute guarantees. But they illustrate how the

2. 21 U.S.C. (1970).

3. 15 U.S.C. §§52–56, 64, 68a–f, 69a–i, 70a–g (1970); 18 U.S.C. §709 (1970).

4. 15 U.S.C. chs. 26, 30, 36.

5. For safety regulation of civil aeronautics, see 49 U.S.C. ch. 20, subch. VI (1970); for ship and boat safety, see 46 U.S.C. ch. 15 (1970), ch. 33 (Supp. IV, 1974); for motor vehicle and highway safety, see 15 U.S.C. ch. 38, and 23 U.S.C. ch. 4 (1970); for railroad safety, see 45 U.S.C. ch. 13 (1970). These statutes and the supplementary administrative regulations issued under their provisions do not comprehend all relevant safety requirements and precautions, but they illustrate this kind of compassionate concern of the federal government.

generous impulses of the government give rise to all sorts of controls.

A host of agencies were created to perform these functions, including the Food and Drug Administration, the Federal Trade Commission, the Consumer Products Safety Commission, the National Transportation Safety Board, inspection services of the Department of Agriculture, and safety divisions in the Interstate Commerce Commission, the Coast Guard, and the Federal Aviation Agency. For each one, pages of statutes brought it into existence, set its mandate, and defined its powers. Each agency discharges its responsibilities through volumes of administrative rules and regulations, orders addressed to individual people and firms, and adjudications of disputed decisions and orders, many of which are reached in courtlike proceedings. For these purposes, each agency has its forms for applications and collecting data, and each issues its own procedural directives. Some agencies have licensing powers, most have powers of inspection, a few have powers of summary action to deal with emergencies.[6] Today, therefore, buyer-seller relations once ignored by the government are modified and controlled by hosts of official specifications and by the public administrative officers and employees who enforce them.

Beyond question, one consequence of all these measures has been to multiply by a large factor the number of governmental constraints people encounter in day-to-day life. Also beyond question, the measures can be traced to entreaties for the protection of people unable to protect themselves in the modern world. This is not to say that every response has been exactly what the petitioners expected or that every response has been a smashing success. But it is from such demands for governmental intercession and from the convergence of political necessity and genuine concern

6. For a survey of the types of adjudicatory actions performed by administrative agencies, see Dalmas H. Nelson, *Administrative Agencies of the U.S.A.* (Wayne State University Press, 1964).

OF OUR OWN MAKING

for innocent victims that the avalanche of government paper often springs.

Buyer-seller relations are only one of the broad areas in which the government has been impelled to intervene. It is also a party to relations between employers and employees and between unions and union members,[7] universities and students,[8] bankrupts and their creditors,[9] tenants and landlords,[10] shippers and carriers,[11] state and local governments and their residents,[12] banks and depositors,[13] investors and issuers and underwriters of securities,[14] lenders and borrowers,[15] researchers and human research subjects,[16] even animal handlers and animals,[17] among many others. It is involved in relations between competing firms of all kinds, both to limit excessive competition for markets and resources and to preserve competition where it is threatened.[18] It is con-

7. 29 U.S.C. chs. 4C, 7–9, 14, 15 (1970), chs. 17–18 (Supp. IV, 1974); 42 U.S.C. ch. 21, subch. VI (1970 and Supp. IV, 1974).
8. For example, the Department of Health, Education, and Welfare issued regulations forbidding colleges and universities to discriminate against women in admissions, financial aid, vocational and academic counseling, and athletics; Nancy Hicks, *New York Times,* June 4, July 19, 1975. Some college administrators protested the growing federal involvement in higher education; Judith Cummings, ibid., November 12 and 16, 1975.
9. 11 U.S.C. chs. 6, 8 (1970).
10. 42 U.S.C. §§3604, 3613 (1970).
11. 49 U.S.C. §§3(1), (2), (3); 20(11), (12); 908; and ch. 4.
12. By statute, public facilities and public education are to be desegregated; 42 U.S.C. §§2000b, 2000c(6) (1970). Also, no program or activity receiving federal financial assistance may discriminate on the ground of race, color, or national origin; 42 U.S.C. §2000d. Federal courts have also held that the Constitution requires correction of gross numerical inequalities in electoral districts at all levels of government; Robert G. Dixon, Jr., *Democratic Representation* (Oxford University Press, 1968).
13. 12 U.S.C. §§371a, b (1970). These provisions apply only to banks that are members of the Federal Reserve System.
14. 15 U.S.C. ch. 2A. See also chs. 2B-1, 2D.
15. 15 U.S.C. ch. 41; 12 U.S.C. ch. 27 (Supp. IV, 1974).
16. 45 C.F.R. pt. 46 (1976).
17. 7 U.S.C. ch. 54 (1970).
18. See, for example, Marle Fainsod, Lincoln Gordon, and Joseph C. Palamountain, Jr., *Government and the American Economy,* 3d ed. (Norton, 1959), pts. 3–5; Alfred E. Kahn, *The Economics of Regulation* (Wiley, 1970), vol. 2, chap. 5.

33

cerned with prices and rates,[19] the quality of goods and services,[20] safety,[21] and equal rights under law.[22] Every such interposition is a response to a cry for help from some group unable to defend its interests by itself. And every one entails as much legislation, administrative procedure and action, and litigation as does intervention in buyer-seller relations. In this sense, much of the great volume of governmental requirements and prohibitions that we encounter on all sides owes its existence to the government's endeavors to keep some people from being hurt by other people.

Alleviating Distress

The government has also responded to pleas for assistance from people buffeted not so much by their fellows as by forces over which they have no control. For a long time, many of these unfortunates were left to the mercy of their families and neighbors, of private charities, of local units of government, or simply of fate; the federal government assumed almost no responsibility for them. But the scale and character of hardship in modern industrial society overwhelmed the traditional instrumentalities of aid. Political pressure, humanitarian impulses, guilt, pity, and other sentiments built up. The federal government could not ignore them; it moved in to help.

Seamen were treated as "wards" of the government early

19. In addition to the types of controls described in the two books cited in n. 18, there is a wide range of controls on financial institutions; see President's Commission on Financial Structure and Regulation, *Report* (GPO, 1972).
20. See, for example, consumer protections in 15 U.S.C. ch. 47. Also, the safety regulations under the laws identified in n. 5, above, include standards and requirements for operators of certain vehicles in interstate commerce and certain repair and training services; see, for example, 14 C.F.R. ch. 1, subchs. D, G, H (1977). On the other hand, see Kahn, *Economics of Regulation,* pp. 21–25, for an argument that quality of service is often ignored.
21. In addition to the safety provisions described in n. 5, above, see Occupational Safety and Health Act, 29 U.S.C. ch. 15 (1970).
22. 42 U.S.C. §§2000e–2000e(17) (1970); 29 U.S.C. ch. 14 (1970).

in the nation's history,[23] as Indians were later.[24] Assistance to veterans and their families was likewise begun many years ago.[25] Later, there were also federal services for children, for the aged, the blind, the disabled, retired workers, the poor, and others.[26] Relief for the victims of natural disasters—floods, droughts, storms, earthquakes—was routinized.[27] Unemployment compensation was federally encouraged and financed by federal grants to tide the unemployed over hard times.[28] The list goes on and on; the federal government has heeded many calls for help.

The government's generosity, incidentally, is not confined to the destitute and the handicapped. Subsidies to farmers and certain industries relieve the hardships of these groups, some of whom would otherwise be forced out of business by foreign competition or adverse economic conditions.[29] State and local governments have also been helped by federal

23. Special legislation governing the rights and duties of seamen go all the way back to the first Congress; 1 Stat. 131. The legislation on the subject has now grown to substantial proportions; 46 U.S.C. ch. 18 (1970).

24. Wilfred E. Binkley and Malcolm C. Moos, *A Grammar of American Politics* (Knopf, 1949), p. 681. The special status of Indians apparently came about because they were considered "conquered nations to whom the United States owed protection under its signed treaties"; Sar A. Levitan and William B. Johnston, *Indian Giving* (Johns Hopkins University Press, 1975), p. 5. For this and other reasons, the government's solicitude seemed to Indians more oppressive than protective. Nevertheless, the Indians are among the first groups for whom a special agency was established and special services maintained; see Alan L. Sorkin, *American Indians and Federal Aid* (Brookings Institution, 1971).

25. President's Commission on Veterans' Pensions, *Staff Report No. 1: The Historical Development of Veterans' Benefits in the United States*, prepared for the House Committee on Veterans' Affairs, 84:2 (GPO, 1956).

26. Gilbert Y. Steiner, *Social Insecurity* (Rand McNally, 1966), *The State of Welfare* (Brookings Institution, 1971), and *The Children's Cause* (Brookings Institution, 1976), chap. 1.

27. Disaster Relief Act of 1970, 84 Stat. 1744. See also "Disaster Assistance," *1975/76 United States Government Manual*, p. 813.

28. William Haber and Merrill G. Murray, *Unemployment Insurance in the American Economy* (Richard D. Irwin, 1966), chaps. 2, 6, 7.

29. *1969 Listing of Operating Federal Assistance Programs Compiled During the Roth Study*, H. Doc. 91-177, 91:1 (GPO, 1969), describes 1,315 aid programs.

grants-in-aid and revenue sharing.[30] Programs on behalf of these beneficiaries are frequently justified in economic rather than moral terms—the supports presumably enable important functions to continue and also preserve the jobs these functions create. But welfare programs for the poor may be similarly defended on economic grounds, for they shore up purchasing power and thus provide job-sustaining, production-maintaining markets. The philosophical differences between services to various target populations are quite narrow. *All* these services come about because people and organizations in distress seek federal contributions to alleviate their pain, and the federal government, for a mixture of pragmatic and idealistic reasons, answers the calls.

The moment a government program for a specified group gets started, legislation and administrative directives and court battles proliferate. It is essential to define who is in the group and who is not. The amounts of benefits and the criteria for determining who in the group is eligible for which amount must be established. Procedures for requesting benefits, for processing such applications, for distributing the benefits, and for settling disputes with applicants over their entitlements have to be set up. Preparations must be made to defend actions in court and to justify them to legislators representing disappointed constituents. In short, because each decision in a grant program is tailored to the situation of each recipient, the administering agencies are compelled to issue a multitude of guidelines and to construct elaborate machinery to accomplish their ends.

30. Such aid programs serve many purposes besides providing support; see V. O. Key, *The Administration of Federal Grants to the States* (Public Administration Service, 1937), pp. 1–26; Committee on Federal Grants-in-Aid, Council of State Governments, *Federal Grants-in-Aid* (CSG, 1949), pp. 42–43; Walter W. Heller and Joseph A. Pechman, "Questions and Answers on Revenue Sharing," in *Revenue Sharing and Its Alternatives: What Future for Fiscal Federalism?* Hearings before the Subcommittee on Fiscal Policy of the Joint Economic Committee, 90:1 (GPO, 1967), pp. 111–17 (Brookings Reprint 135). Beyond question, however, helping state and local governments meet their obligations to their citizens and creditors is one of the major objectives.

OF OUR OWN MAKING

Consider a couple of illustrations from social security. The statute provides for "mother's insurance benefits." A number of conditions must be met for a woman to qualify, including one that she have "in her care a child of the deceased worker under age 18 or disabled who is entitled to child's insurance benefits." But what does "in her care" mean? Some women apply even though they are not living with the child in question; must the mother and child be living together? Is living together proof that the child is in her care? Does legal right to the child's care and custody by itself establish eligibility? Nearly two pages of regulations have been promulgated to answer questions of this kind for all foreseeable contingencies in connection with this single phrase. ("In her care" means that she exercises "parental control and responsibility for the welfare and care" of the child, or performs "personal services" for a child eighteen or over who is mentally incompetent.[31] Parental control and responsibility, in turn, mean "supervising the child's activities and participating in the important decisions about the child's physical and mental needs."[32] Performing personal services means "services [with illustrations listed] performed for a child other than any routine household services which are performed for any adult member of a household."[33] Parental control and responsibility may be exercised indirectly, with mother and child apart, but for specified lengths of time and for specific purposes, such as the child being away at school.[34] Mere legal right to a child's care and custody does not in itself constitute parental care and responsibility.[35] Indeed, there is a whole section illustrating situations in which a mother is deemed *not* to have a child in her care.[36]) It is necessary to go on at such length and in such detail because thousands of employees of the

31. 20 C.F.R. pt. 404.342 (1976).
32. 20 C.F.R. pt. 404.345.
33. 20 C.F.R. pt. 404.344.
34. 20 C.F.R. pts. 404.347, 404.348.
35. 20 C.F.R. pt. 404.343(a)(2).
36. 20 C.F.R. pt. 404.349.

37

Social Security Administration must make judgments on tens of thousands of claims encompassing all sorts of different circumstances. Only precise, specific guidelines can assure common treatment of like cases. Otherwise, programs for alleviating distress on an individual basis lose all consistency.

Similarly, the statutory provisions for disability payments under the social security program are amplified by a large body of administrative regulations. Disability is defined in the legislation as "inability to engage in any substantial gainful activity by reason of any medically determinable physical or mental impairment which can be expected to result in death or has lasted or can be expected to last for a continuous period of not less than 12 months."[37] But it takes fifteen pages of specifications of symptoms, clinical signs, and laboratory findings for the musculoskeletal system, special sense organs, respiratory system, cardiovascular system, digestive system, genitourinary system, hemic and lymphatic system, skin, endocrine system, multiple body systems, neurological problems, mental disorders, and malignant neoplastic diseases to describe the kinds of impairments within the statutory standard.[38] Indeed, even when the statute is quite specific ("'blindness' means central visual acuity of 20/200 or less in the better eye with the use of a correcting lens. An eye which is accompanied by a limitation in the fields of vision such that the widest diameter of the visual field subtends an angle no greater than 20 degrees shall be considered for the purposes of this paragraph as having a central visual acuity of 20/200 or less"[39]), it may require elaboration. In the case of blindness, administrative regulations prescribe the tests to be used in determining visual acuity—for instance, for an eye with a lens, the "usual perimetric methods, utilizing a 3 mm. white disc target at a distance of 330 mm. under illumination

37. 20 C.F.R. pt. 404.1501(a)(i).
38. 20 C.F.R. pt. 404, subpt. P, appendix.
39. 42 U.S.C. §416(i)(1)(B) (1970).

of not less than 7 foot-candles," according to a prescribed table of central visual efficiency and a chart showing the normal field of vision and the method of computing percentage of field efficiency.[40] In this fashion, the Social Security Administration tries to make sure that the same criteria of eligibility are applied everywhere.

Obviously, the program could be run with far fewer specifications and requirements. One consequence, however, would be the award of benefits to people whom Congress and the program administrators never intended to support and the denial of benefits to many they wanted to reach. Once a program of tailor-made assistance gets started, it is not likely to attain its announced objectives unless it is laid out in great detail. Humane goals thus add to the paper blizzard.

Forestalling Systemic Disruptions

Another way in which the federal government strives to prevent pain and hardship from afflicting people is by heading off systemic breakdowns. Industrial systems are composed of such specialized and interdependent subsystems that a failure of any subsystem inevitably slows or stops other subsystems, and the repercussions spread through the whole society. If the subsystem is an especially important one—transportation, energy, agriculture, or a basic industry like steel production—the results can be catastrophic. Many federal interventions in the economy, with their accompanying mounds of laws and regulations, are brought on by the resolve to shield people from the suffering that would ensue.

Hence the programs and agencies to prevent work stoppages caused by labor-management and interunion disputes,[41]

40. Ibid., table 2, n. 1.
41. The agencies set up for this purpose include the Federal Labor Relations Council, the Federal Mediation and Conciliation Service, the Federal Service Impasses Panel, the National Labor Relations Board, the National Mediation Board, and of course the Department of Labor; *1975/76 United States Government Manual*, p. 817.

to manage the economy when inflation or deflation threatens its stability,[42] to prevent the waste and destruction of natural resources and to assure a steady supply of vital materials from abroad,[43] to deter aggression against this country and its friends by potential foes,[44] to assist other nations striving for economic and political development and stability,[45] and to encourage and facilitate the peaceful resolution of international conflicts that could explode into worldwide crises.[46] Even leaders whose personal preference might be to stay aloof from such involvements cannot ignore the demands and expectations of the people generally, or of powerful groups among them, that the government do something about such dangers. The government will therefore almost always do something—maybe something that proves unwise in retrospect, but in any case, something—to forestall events and

42. The Economic Policy Council, the Council on International Economic Policy, the President's Economic Policy Board, the United States International Trade Commission, the Council on Wage and Price Stability, the Council of Economic Advisers, the Federal Reserve System, elements of the Departments of the Treasury and Commerce, and others; ibid., p. 814.

43. For illustrations, see the agencies listed in ibid. under "Agriculture and Agricultural Programs" (p. 811), "Conservation" (p. 812), "Electric Power" (p. 814), "Energy" (pp. 814–15), "Environmental Protection" (p. 815), "Fish and Fisheries" (p. 815), "Flood Control" (p. 815), "Forest and Forest Products" (p. 816), "Imports and Exports" (p. 817), "Land" (p. 817), "Mining" (p. 819), "Nuclear Energy" (p. 819), "Oceans" (p. 819), "Oil" (p. 819), "Pollution" (p. 820), "Recreation" (p. 820), "Tariffs" (p. 821), "Textiles" (p. 822), "Tobacco and Tobacco Products" (p. 822), "Trade" (p. 822), "Water and Waterways" (pp. 822–23), and "Wildlife" (p. 823).

44. This includes not only the Departments of Defense and State, but all the international defense organizations to which the United States belongs, the intelligence-gathering agencies, the Arms Control and Disarmament Agency, and the emergency preparedness programs throughout the government; ibid., "Defense, National," p. 813, and "Emergency Preparedness," p. 814. See also n. 45, below.

45. To get an idea of the varieties of programs of this kind, see *The Foreign Assistance Program: Annual Report* [of the President] *to the Congress for Fiscal Year 1971*.

46. In addition to unilateral mediation efforts by the Secretary of State and other representatives of the President, the United States belongs to more than two dozen multilateral international organizations of a nonmilitary character; *1975/76 United States Government Manual*, pp. 653–64.

practices that could disrupt the system under which we live.

Of course, the programs launched to provide this security increase the size of the government and the number and complexity of government operations and procedures. Think of the number of agencies set up to work for the objectives just mentioned: the Department of Labor, the National Labor Relations Board, the National Mediation Board, the Federal Mediation and Conciliation Service, the Department of the Interior, the Environmental Protection Agency, the Federal Energy Administration, the Energy Research and Development Administration, the Department of Commerce, the Department of State, the Agency for International Development, the Export-Import Bank, the Department of Defense, the Central Intelligence Agency, and many others. If we were willing to take greater risks with the very existence of our economic and political systems, we would undoubtedly enjoy less government, smaller government, and simpler government—provided, that is, we had any government at all. Perhaps we have opted for excessive caution. But the suffering from systemic breakdowns evidently is so much less acceptable than the controls and procedures set up to prevent them that we prefer the certain constraints and annoyances to the possibility of even temporary disruption.

Compassion and Expedience

In suggesting that there is compassion behind governmental policies intended to protect people from one another, help the victims of events that overwhelm them, and keep the system from breaking down or being smashed, I don't mean to rule out the political expediency of these policies. The careers, reputations, even the jobs of government officers and employees depend on the maintenance of order and continuity in the polity; if substantial numbers of people—even if they are only a minority—are disaffected and rebellious or if the society cannot function or defend itself, the institutions of government may be overturned, sweeping the leaders out.

41

And even if the institutions survive, the leaders will be replaced if they appear indifferent to the pains and fears of the public. So it is in the self-interest of officials to respond to people's expressions of distress and anxiety. Compassion and expediency thus converge to produce the proliferation of government requirements, prohibitions, and labyrinthine procedures.

REPRESENTATIVENESS AND ITS CONSEQUENCES

Despite governmental solicitude, distrust of government is a deeply ingrained tradition in America. Consequently, the growth of government stimulates fear in the people even though the growth came about in response to demands for protection and assistance from the people themselves. Americans worry about the dangers of tyranny or at least of official arrogance. And they are uneasy about the possibility that the vast impersonal machinery of government, with its endless obscure activities and powers, will be turned from its public purposes to private advantage by powerful private interests or crooks in its ranks or outside. That is, Americans assert a need to be protected *from* the government as well as *by* it, and they recognize a need to protect *it* from those who would despoil it.

The representativeness of the government is a safeguard against such abuses. If all interests are represented in the government's decisionmaking processes and if its decisions are not skewed by resources or methods employed only by a small set of interests, it is less likely to be tyrannical, arbitrary, dishonest, or extensively victimized. So steps have been taken to assure representativeness.

Unfortunately, like so many other unexceptionable objectives, this one too brings procedural complications, substantive constraints, paperwork, and additional agencies in its wake. How these undesired characteristics are brought about by the quest for representativeness is best explained by examining some of the specific tactics employed in that quest. Efforts to guarantee due process, rationality in decisionmaking, the integrity of every decision, and taxation with representation illustrate clearly what happens.

Due Process

Preservation of due process, for instance, obliges officials to give people affected by governmental actions a fair chance to get their views on official decisions registered so that their interests are not overlooked or arbitrarily overridden by those in power. Actions judged to be in violation of these requirements may be nullified.

The desire for fairness adds to the practices and constraints commonly regarded as red tape. Take the Administrative Procedure Act as an example.[47] Enacted in 1946, it is a legally binding codification and summary of procedural fairness requirements governing administrative agencies. It applies to agency rules ("the whole or any part of any agency statement of general or particular applicability and future effect"), orders ("the whole or any part of the final disposition . . . of any agency in any matter other than rule making but including licensing"), and licenses ("the whole or part of any agency permit, certificate, approval, registration, charter, membership, statutory exemption or other form of permission"), and to the processes by which each of these decisions is reached and promulgated.[48]

To ensure that people are not kept in the dark about who is responsible for the decisions about rules, orders, and licenses, by what authority the decisions are issued, the exact wording of the decisions, and how and where to protest unfavorable decisions, the statute includes a section on public information commanding agencies to "separately state and

47. 60 Stat. 237; now incorporated, as amended, in 5 U.S.C. ch. 5, subch. II, and ch. 7 (1970 and Supp. IV, 1974).
48. 5 U.S.C. §551 (1970 and Supp. IV, 1974).

currently publish in the Federal Register" descriptions of central and field organization, including delegations of authority; "statements of the general course and methods by which its functions are channeled and determined," including formal or informal procedures and forms and instructions; and substantive rules plus statements of general policy or interpretations adopted by the agencies. They must also "publish or, in accordance with published rule, make available to public inspection all final opinions or orders in the adjudication of cases." Matters of record must, in accordance with published rules, be made available to "persons properly and directly concerned."[49]

Another section of the law, on rule making, requires also that "general notice of proposed rule making shall be published in the Federal Register," and that each agency "shall afford interested persons an opportunity to participate in the rule making" through written submissions "with or without opportunity to present the same orally." All relevant submissions must be considered by the decisionmakers, and rules adopted must contain "a concise general statement of their basis and purpose." Any interested person must be accorded "the right to petition for the issuance, amendment, or repeal of a rule."[50]

Small wonder, then, that the *Federal Register* and the *Code of Federal Regulations* fill shelf after shelf in library stacks.

The act also specifies how various proceedings must be conducted. A section on adjudication directs that persons entitled to notice of an agency hearing be given timely information about all the relevant details of the pending matter. The times and places of hearings must be set "with due regard . . . for the convenience and necessity of the parties or their representatives." Agencies must give all interested parties a chance for "the submission and consideration of facts, arguments,

49. 5 U.S.C. §552 (1970 and Supp. IV, 1974).
50. 5 U.S.C. §553 (1970 and Supp. IV, 1974).

offers of settlement, or proposals of adjustment," and, if no agreement is reached, a chance for a hearing.[51]

The management of hearings is spelled out in detail, with particulars on the powers of presiding officers, the taking of evidence (including the right to cross-examine), and the character of the official record. Decisions by subordinates are authorized, but appeal to "the agency" (i.e., its highest officers) is permitted, and the procedures for appeal are explicitly described. Decisions must include "findings and conclusions, as well as the reasons or basis therefor, upon all the material issues of fact, law, or discretion presented on the record." Agencies are directed to appoint "as many qualified and competent examiners [now called administrative law judges] as may be necessary" for these purposes.[52]

Finally, "Any person suffering legal wrong because of any agency action, or adversely affected or aggrieved by such action . . . shall be entitled to judicial review thereof." Review proceedings and the scope of court jurisdiction are defined.[53]

Here, then, are some of the reasons for the elaborateness and deliberateness of administrative procedures in federal agencies. To be sure, were there no Administrative Procedure Act, agencies would not cavalierly trample the rights of their clients; other statutes, judicial precedents, political pressures, and generally accepted standards of equity would keep them in check. But the act unquestionably compelled them to formalize and elaborate their procedures to a greater degree than they otherwise would.

Special due-process guarantees cover employees of the government.[54] Superiors cannot hire and fire subordinates at will, punish them freely, or even unrestrainedly assign them to functions or locations. Civil service laws and regulations, collective bargaining agreements, and, more recently, judicial

51. 5 U.S.C. §554 (1970).
52. 5 U.S.C. §556 (1970).
53. 5 U.S.C. §§701–06 (1970).
54. 5 U.S.C. chs. 33, 35, 71–77 (1970); 5 C.F.R. (1977).

interpretations of the first amendment to the Constitution,[55] not to mention political realities, circumscribe the superiors, and aggrieved employees may seek formal review of actions affecting them. At least some of the slowness, awkwardness, and intricacy of federal administration can be traced to the protection of the rights of people who work for the government.

A society less concerned about the rights of individuals in government and out might well be governed with a much smaller volume of paper and much simpler and faster administrative procedures than are typical of governance in this country. Americans have adopted a different mix.

Representation, Rationality, and Administrative Effectiveness

Participation of relevant interests in decisionmaking, one of the principal ways of achieving due process, is an end in itself. At the same time, it contributes to another widely shared value, rationality in decisionmaking. Rationality, in turn, is both an end in itself and a means to another value, administrative effectiveness. The simultaneous pursuit of all these objectives generates still more of the practices and requirements reviled as red tape.

Rationality here refers to consideration of all reasonable alternatives and their effects when choices must be made. It also refers to the logical consistency of decisions, to the elimination of inexplicable and unjustifiable discrepancies among them, and to the avoidance of embarrassing contradictions.

Lack of comprehensiveness in weighing alternatives can reduce rationality and effectiveness in several ways. It may result in selection of a course of action inferior to other available options. It may eventuate in decisions that powerful public agencies and political leaders, excluded from the process of deciding, cannot support. It may produce policies offensive to a segment of the community capable of offering

55. *Elrod* v. *Burns*, 452 U.S. 909 (1976).

strong resistance and even of overturning them. In short, wisdom, teamwork, and compliance may suffer from the failure to take into account everything and everybody that reasonably could be taken into account in arriving at a policy position.

Lack of consistency can reduce rationality and effectiveness in similar ways. The work of one agency may end up negating the labors of another. The discovery by some people that other people in the same position fare better because different agencies or regional offices handle identical problems in different ways may lead to noncompliance, litigation, and even political upheavals. Indeed, inconsistent requirements may force citizens to violate some legal mandates in order to comply with others, which means that one or more programs will fall short of their announced goals. In any event, disclosure of such cases makes those in power look ludicrous.

Government procedures were therefore designed to avert these doleful possibilities by facilitating interest-group participation in official decisions to a greater extent than would be dictated by concern for fairness alone. This makes it harder to reach policy decisions. But giving every interested party a voice in official decisions increases the likelihood that no feasible option will be overlooked, that no important consequence of any feasible option will be forgotten or unperceived, that conflicts and contradictions will be brought to light and resolved, and that the policies ultimately emerging from such broadly reviewed deliberations will enjoy a higher degree of voluntary compliance on the part of the public than policies fashioned in ignorance of public attitudes and expectations. Presumably, such policies will also be maximally fair because nobody's rights are likely to be trampled under these conditions. Whether they are more just or not, however, they are said to enjoy better hope of success than policies formulated in isolation or secrecy. It is in this sense that they are called more rational and effective.

Some of the methods of increasing group participation are time-honored.[56] One is to designate agencies to be spokesmen for specific groups; at the departmental level, for example, the Departments of Labor, Agriculture, and Commerce were so conceived, but there are also many single-constituency agencies at the bureau level and among the so-called independent bodies, such as the Veterans' Administration. Other long-standing methods include selecting agency staffs from the clientele served or regulated and reserving places on administrative and advisory boards for representatives of such interests. Occasionally, a private interest may be virtually clothed with public authority. These practices are often assailed for giving too much weight to special interests as against the public interest, and their efficacy in furthering the cause of justice and rationality has been sharply questioned. Hidden motives may indeed underlie some of them. All the same, they doubtless do result in decisions different from the ones public officials would reach if nongovernmental groups had no part in official decisionmaking. That is why they were invented and why they endure.

More recently, interest-group representation has been pressed into new areas. In the war against poverty, particularly, the federal government insisted that federally assisted local antipoverty agencies include the poor and ethnic minorities in their governing boards, while some revenue sharing programs require evidence of local participation in the drafting of applications for federal funds.[57]

56. Avery Leiserson, "Interest Groups in Administration," in Fritz Morstein Marx, ed., *Elements of Public Administration* (Prentice-Hall, 1946).

57. Joseph A. Kershaw, *Government Against Poverty* (Brookings Institution, 1970), pp. 45–47; and Herbert Kaufman, "Administrative Decentralization and Political Power," *Public Administration Review*, vol. 29 (January–February 1969), pp. 3–15. For the provisions for citizen participation in community development grant applications, see 42 U.S.C. §5304(a)(6) (Supp. IV, 1974). See also the steps taken by the Secretary of Health, Education, and Welfare to increase the public's role in the formulation of departmental regulations; Eric Wentworth, *Washington Post*, July 25, 1976.

Old or new, the methods of interest-group representation generate more directives and controls, more steps in the forging of governmental policies, more bargaining before decisions are reached, and more postdecision litigation than would otherwise develop. Fairness, comprehensiveness, and community acceptance of policy decisions obviously rate higher than administrative simplicity and speed.

Increased participation in governmental decisions by external groups is matched by procedures to make sure that every administrative unit *inside* the government also contributes its special knowledge, point of view, and sympathy for its clientele to the final product. One method is compulsory clearance of pending decisions with every relevant organizational unit whose jurisdiction touches on the matters under consideration; the Secretary of Housing and Urban Development, for instance, is forbidden by the Housing and Community Development Act of 1974 to make community development grants "unless the application therefor has been submitted for review and comment to an areawide agency under procedures established by the President,"[58] while the State Department, according to one report, has developed clearance to such a high art that as many as twenty-seven signatures may be required on an instruction to an ambassador before it is sent.[59] Another method is to require studies and written reports on various "impacts" of proposed policies; environmental impact statements are now mandatory prerequisites for official action affecting the environment, inflation impact statements must accompany draft legislation, rules, and regulations proposed by executive branch agencies, and similar statements about the consequences of pending measures for the public's paperwork burdens, for the costs

58. 42 U.S.C. §5304(e) (Supp. IV, 1974).
59. Terence Smith, "Foreign Policy: Ebbing of Power at the State Department," *New York Times*, January 17, 1971; cited in John H. Esterline and Robert B. Black, *Inside Foreign Policy* (Mayfield Publishing, 1975), p. 60, footnote.

of doing business, and for family life have been proposed.[60] Still another method is to place separate organizations under a common command with authority to compel coordination.[61] All these devices are internal counterparts of external-group representation and are defended with the same arguments: fewer vital considerations are neglected, less opposition and evasion are engendered.

Opinions about the effectualness of these practices vary. But even if they accomplish all that is claimed for them, there is a cost in "red tape." They multiply the paper flow inside the system or the paperwork demands on the public or both. They make the government slow and ponderous, thus reducing the vigor of policy execution. They increase expenses. Sometimes unknowingly or unwillingly, but often deliberately, we pay these costs to get the asserted benefits even if the costs are certain and the benefits in doubt.

Keeping Government Public

Similarly, we try to do whatever is necessary to keep the government from turning into an instrumentality of private profit for those in its employ or those with private fortunes at their disposal.

60. The guidelines for environmental impact statements are in 40 C.F.R. pt. 1500 (1976). Inflation impact statements are mandated in Executive Order 11821 (November 27, 1974), as extended by Executive Order 11949 (December 31, 1976). The proposal for paperwork impact findings is in *The Federal Paperwork Burden*, S. Rept. 93-125, 93:1 (1973), pp. 69–71. The case for family impact statements is advanced in Sheila B. Kamerman, *Developing a Family Impact Statement*, An Occasional Paper from the Foundation for Child Development (New York: FCD, May 1976). A plan for economic impact statements describing the costs that would be imposed on business by proposed administrative regulations reportedly provoked controversy among top government officials; David Burnham, *New York Times*, May 9, 1977.

61. Hierarchy is probably the oldest axiom of organization; see Exodus 19:25. It is usually justified on grounds of coordination; for example, see Leonard D. White, *Introduction to the Study of Public Administration*, 4th ed. (Macmillan, 1955), pp. 38–39; and Herbert A. Simon, Donald W. Smithburg, and Victor A. Thompson, *Public Administration* (Knopf, 1950), pp. 130–33. When reorganizers speak of "streamlining" administration, they usually mean grouping agencies in larger collectivities under a single command, the way the armed services, once separate from each other, were gathered under the Department of Defense.

The temptations facing the government work force are varied and enormous. They handle hundreds of billions of dollars in revenues, in expenditures (paychecks, retirement benefits, payments for supplies and services, rent, subsidies, tax refunds, etc.), and in vast quantities of removable property, from postage stamps and office equipment to vehicles and electronic gear. Without exceedingly tight controls, nobody would ever know if one government employee took a little here, another stole a little there, and a third pocketed a bit somewhere else. Public moneys would thus be diverted from their intended uses to the enrichment of dishonest public servants. Even if no individual defalcation were large, the collective effect could be massive.[62] And without controls, unfortunately, the scale of the average individual offense would doubtless be substantial.

Public officers and employees are also tempted by opportunities to sell their official discretion and information.[63]

62. Some indication of possible scale is provided by the experience of retail stores. Despite $2 billion spent annually for security, stores lost almost $6 billion to thieves, and experts estimated that three-quarters of all thefts were committed by employees; *U.S. News & World Report* (June 16, 1975), p. 28. The National Retail Merchants Association offered a somewhat lower estimate, but one still in excess of a billion dollars a year taken by employees; *Newsweek* (November 24, 1975), pp. 103, 107.

63. Not a year goes by without at least a few such cases coming to light. In 1974, for example, the Supreme Court upheld the conviction of a former immigration officer for accepting bribes (and for other crimes) while in office (Warren Weaver, Jr., *New York Times*, February 26); a congressman pleaded guilty to charges of accepting fees while in office to represent a company in dealings with federal agencies from which it was seeking favorable decisions (Arnold H. Lubasch, *NYT*, October 2); and a former import specialist with the Customs Bureau went to prison after pleading guilty to accepting gifts from art galleries (*NYT*, October 5). In 1975, a high-ranking officer of the Small Business Administration was arrested for accepting bribes and other offenses (*NYT*, April 12); seven employees of the Immigration and Naturalization Service were convicted of a series of crimes, including encouraging and assisting illegal entry into the country and drug smuggling (*NYT*, October 5, 1974, and M. A. Farber, *NYT*, April 27, 1975); another INS officer pleaded guilty to taking bribes to give permanent status to aliens working as waiters in restaurants, including three owned by the defendant (Donald Janson, *NYT*, July 1; and *NYT*, November 27); a retired collection officer of the Internal Revenue Service was indicted for soliciting and receiving bribes for favors to taxpayers (Max H. Siegel, *NYT*, October 25); a Federal Energy Administration official was arrested for requesting a bribe from a coal

Historically, the letting of government contracts, the sale or gift of government land, and the disposition of government-owned resources were riddled with corruption of this kind as government agents were bribed to overlook wholesale perversions of the law. Indeed, some inspectors and law-enforcement officers and tax collectors in all fields have occasionally been induced to disregard violations, withhold reports to higher levels, or at least reduce charges against offenders. They have also been persuaded to certify that products of substandard quality meet legal specifications and that extravagant tax deductions are valid. They have been paid to leak confidential information enabling their corrupters to beat out competitors in the marketplace or in bidding for government contracts, or even allowing foreign governments to gain an advantage over our own.

They have also been tempted by the opportunities to extort payments.[64] Permits can be delayed, licenses held up, deliberations protracted, proceedings prolonged, unless re-

---

brokerage company to reverse a decision (*NYT*, November 7); and a financial aid officer in the Department of Health, Education, and Welfare resigned under congressional investigation for alleged acceptance of bribes to approve student loans to a chain of vocational education schools accused of cheating both students and the federal government of student aid funds (Nancy Hicks, *NYT*, November 20). In 1976, an assistant secretary of the Department of Housing and Urban Development resigned at the request of the President while under investigation for exploring future job possibilities with firms doing business with his department (Philip Shabecoff, *NYT*, January 29); the President withdrew his nominee for assistant secretary of the Air Force when it was disclosed that the nominee had been promised a job by a major defense contractor after the end of his government service (*NYT*, March 26); contract officers in the Department of Defense were found to have taken favors from contractors ("U.S. Government Employees and Officials, Ethics in Office," *New York Times Index*, entry for July 5); and Defense Department meat inspectors admitted to a congressional committee that they took bribes from meat suppliers to misgrade meat sold to the military (Morton Mintz, *Washington Post*, May 7, and Spencer Rich, *Washington Post*, May 11). The list, unfortunately, is lengthy.

64. For example, a former agent of the Alcohol, Tobacco, and Firearms Bureau was indicted for extortion (*New York Times*, June 15, 1974), and a quality-assurance specialist of the General Services Administration was convicted of exacting kickbacks for contracts (ibid., January 8, 1976).

wards are offered. Inspectors can charge violations by the score if their requests for payoffs are rejected. At one time, government workers were fired if they did not contribute to the political party in power, and parties routinely attracted people to toil for them free by holding out the hope of eventual government employment as compensation.

We have attempted to suppress such practices. Many of them, such as bribery, have been declared crimes, but criminal penalties deter only if there is a good chance that the forbidden acts will be detected. Corrupt bargains, however, are difficult to detect. We have therefore gone beyond deterrence; we have tried, by elaborate procedural safeguards, to make the commission of these acts almost impossible. These tactics are executed through torrents of laws and regulations and cumbersome procedures; it is sometimes said the prevention costs more than the ailment. But our attitude toward public property is typified by the comments of a famous economist ordinarily inclined to reject costs that exceed benefits in dollar terms: "The Office of Management and Budget *should* spend $20 to prevent the theft of $1 of public funds."[65] Not only are public property and public discretion held to have a special moral status; they occupy a special political position because abusing them eats away at the foundations of representative government. So we are willing to put up with a lot to safeguard their integrity.

The controls on accounting and financial management therefore abound,[66] as do the statutes and regulations on per-

65. Arthur M. Okun, *Equality and Efficiency: The Big Tradeoff* (Brookings Institution, 1975), p. 60.

66. See, for example, 31 U.S.C. chs. 1A, 2, 10, 18 (1970); 4 C.F.R. (1977); and the entries under "Accounts and Accounting" in the General Index, U.S.C.S. (Lawyer's Ed., 1973). There are also many internal documents governing financial management, such as the Federal Management Circulars of the Office of Management and Budget; see 34 C.F.R. ch. I (1976). Among the executive departments and agencies of the federal government (not including government corporations and certain quasi-governmental bodies), 286 accounting systems are currently in use; [*Sixth*] *Report by the Comptroller General of the United States on the Status, Progress, and Problems in Federal Agency Accounting during Fiscal Year 1975*, pp. 1–5.

sonnel administration,[67] on government contracting and procurement,[68] on property management,[69] on data processing,[70] on privacy and freedom of information.[71] There are watchdogs who watch watchdogs watching watchdogs. The Treasury, the Office of Management and Budget, and the General Accounting Office stand guard over fiscal matters, along with departmental and bureau financial officers. The Civil Service Commission and departmental and bureau personnel administrators are the guardians of the personnel system. The General Services Administration maintains surveillance over purchasing and property, the Office of Management and Budget over agency compliance with privacy laws, and the Attorney General over freedom of information practices. Though every agency has its own legal counsel, only the Department of Justice (with a few exceptions) represents the government in court.

Administrators of line agencies chafe at these restraints, the paperwork they inflict, the time and frustration they add to the routine business of government. Chances are that most of the public knows little about them, though anyone who does business with the government doubtless learns quickly. Much of the often-satirized clumsiness, slowness, and complexity of government procedures is merely the consequence of all these precautions. Things would be simpler and faster if we were not resolved to block abuses that turn public goods to private profit.

67. 5 U.S.C. pts. II, III (1970); 5 C.F.R. pts. 1–1300, 1501 (1977). In addition to nearly 300 pages of legislation and over 400 pages of rules and regulations applicable to the whole government, each agency has its own personnel manual.

68. 41 U.S.C. (1970); 41 C.F.R. subtitles A, B (1976).

69. 40 U.S.C. chs. 3, 4, 6, 10, 11, 12, 14, 15, 16 (1970): 41 C.F.R. subtitle C (1976).

70. 40 U.S.C. §759; 34 C.F.R. pt. 281 (1976); 41 C.F.R. pt. 101-32.

71. Privacy Act of 1974 (88 Stat. 1896); Freedom of Information Act (81 Stat. 54, amended in 88 Stat. 1561). See also C.F.R. Index, "Privacy Act" and "Information Availability." [These sources and related text corrected from first printing.]

"Name and address? I knew it—I knew there'd be a lot of red tape!"

A private redirection of government occurs also when rich people and organizations successfully use their wealth to determine who gets office or what the officeholders do. Such uses of wealth were not held illegal or immoral in the past; they were taken for granted. But the disparities in wealth in the society give to the rich an advantage in selecting leaders and controlling official behavior out of all proportion to their numbers. These inequalities conflict with the ideal that each individual should carry as nearly as possible the same political weight as every other individual. We have therefore taken steps to reduce them. That is why there are laws that limit contributions to political parties and candidates, set ceilings on political campaign expenditures, grant public funds to eligible parties for their nominating and electoral functions,

55

and establish agencies to administer and police these laws.[72] It is also why we oblige lobbyists to register and to disclose their finances[73] and why there are a constitutional amendment and legislation forbidding denial of the right to vote for nonpayment of poll taxes or other taxes.[74]

Most of these requirements bring in their train a good deal of red tape for those to whom they apply. They mean people and organizations that used to act without reference to the government at all have to read statutes and regulations, prepare applications, file reports, keep records, appeal unfavorable decisions, and in other ways accommodate themselves to public officials and employees. Many constraints of this sort directly affect only a small percentage of the population. All together, however, they touch large numbers of us. In this way, high idealism precipitates the requirements and prohibitions, the twists and turns in the governmental maze, that contribute to the luxuriant growth of government red tape.

Taxation with Representation

One area in which a noble ideal has resulted in almost *universal* discontent with the voluminousness and complications of government requirements is taxation. Taxation without representation is odious to Americans in principle. Taxation with representation, however, may make for a greater profusion of elaborate and incomprehensible statutes and regulations than one would find in an autocratic system.

For everyone has a finger in the making of our tax policy. Not with perfect equality, of course; differences in influence and in concern are substantial. Directly or indirectly, how-

72. For a full collection of all the relevant statutory provisions, see *Federal Election Campaign Laws*, compiled by the Federal Election Commission, 1976. See also 2 U.S.C. ch. 8 (1970); C.F.R. Index (1976), "Political Activity" and "Political Candidates"; and 41 Fed. Reg. 35932–76 (August 25, 1976).

73. 2 U.S.C. ch. 8A.

74. Twenty-fourth Amendment. See also 42 U.S.C. §1973h (1970) for enforcing legislation.

ever, most interests have some impact on tax decisions. In a society as diversified as ours, that means a lot of fingers.

Indeed, our society is so complex that even an absolute autocrat would have trouble keeping the tax system simple; the economic situations of taxpayers vary so much that only a sophisticated system would be likely to produce large public revenues without devastating large sectors of the economy. Furthermore, taxes are not only instruments for raising money; they are also employed for management of the economy. They can be lowered to encourage certain kinds of activity or to assist growth in certain regions, and raised for the opposite purpose. Increased at strategic times, they can, all other things remaining the same, combat inflationary tendencies; decreased, other things unchanged, they can spur the economy. When all these effects are factored into a tax system, it takes a great deal of legislative and administrative elaboration to make it work.

In a diversified and democratic polity, the system gets still more elaborate as each set of interests strives to shift as much of the tax burden from its own shoulders as it can. Battles may be fought over broad policy issues—sales versus income taxes, the degree of progressivity of income tax schedules, business versus personal income liabilities, payroll taxes versus other methods of financing. Equally important for the complexity of the tax system and the difficulties of complying with its requirements, however, are the large reductions in taxes that some groups enjoy because of relatively small changes in tax laws and regulations. Such provisions often go unnoticed by all who are not affected by them. If they are observed, the observers may agree to withhold opposition and publicity in return for support of their own special advantages. Obscure parts of long technical legislative bills and administrative regulations thus make their way routinely through the policymaking machinery. That is why proposals that begin as comprehensive tax reform usually end up as "Christmas-tree" law—law containing a gift for nearly everyone. Nobody would argue that the results are models of equity and rationality. Certainly, they are far from simple, brief, and symmetrical.[75] Everybody grumbles.

The shortcomings of taxation with representation were probably not fully anticipated by those who struggled for it. Had they been able to see what lay ahead, however, they probably would still have opted for it, shortcomings and all.

DIVERSITY, DISTRUST, AND DEMOCRACY

Americans' insistence on compassionate and representative government thus contributes to the enormous output of requirements and prohibitions and the elaborateness of procedures so characteristic of our political system. Compassion and representativeness are not the only values we pursue, of course; they do not account for the *total* volume of paper and *all* the procedural complexities. We also set great store by efficiency, expertness, vigorous leadership, freedom to do as we please and to be let alone, stability, strength, and other things. Exploring the multifarious effects of only two broad values, however, illustrates how the things we treasure and demand lead to the curtailments of freedom of action, the burdens and inconveniences, and the delays we decry. If these are the consequences of just two values, though they are sweeping ones, imagine the combined impact of all of them.

Were we a less differentiated society, the blizzard of official paper might be less severe and the labyrinths of official processes less tortuous. Had we more trust in one another and in our public officers and employees, we would not feel impelled to limit discretion by means of lengthy, minutely detailed di-

75. See, for instance, the Tax Reform Act of 1976, 90 Stat. 1520, which runs for more than 400 pages. The Internal Revenue Code as a whole, Title 26 of the U.S.C. (1970), goes on for more than 1,000 double-columned pages. The administrative regulations governing internal revenue, Title 26 of the C.F.R. (1976), occupy fourteen volumes and thousands of pages.

"More rules and regulations!"

rectives and prescriptions or to subject public and private actions to check after check. If our polity were less democratic, imperfect though our democracy may be, the government would not respond as readily to the innumerable claims on it for protection and assistance. Diversity, distrust, and democracy thus cause the profusion of constraints and the unwieldiness of the procedures that afflict us. It is in this sense that we bring it on ourselves.

III

Rewinding the Spools

ON THE SURFACE, red tape resembles other noxious by-products we generate in the course of making things and rendering services we are eager to have. More of what we want means more of what we don't want as well. More automobiles mean more pollutants in the air. More electric power means either more air pollution or more radioactive wastes to dispose of, perhaps both. More food means more runoff of fertilizer into our water. More metals and minerals mean more slag heaps. Increased convenience in packaging means more solid refuse. Similarly, it appears, the more values the government tries to advance, the more red tape it inevitably generates.

In some respects, this is a discouraging diagnosis if you want to reduce red tape because it forces hard choices on you. How much of what you want should you give up to lighten your red-tape burdens? Or, to state the dilemma positively, how much red tape should you tolerate to get satisfying amounts of what you want? Cost-benefit analysis helps sharpen the choices, but it cannot make them for you because there is no convincing way to factor in vital intangibles, such as effects on future generations and willingness to take risks. Even more important, each person has his or her own time horizons and schedules of preferences and aversions; what some will surrender willingly others will defend to the death. Getting rid of red tape is therefore a difficult, frustrating undertaking.

But if red tape were really like other harmful by-products of industrial civilizations, a ray of light would brighten this dark picture. Now that the long-range consequences of accumulating industrial by-products are evident, we have begun to concentrate on cutting down on them, recycling them, and disposing of them safely. There is still a long way to go, and we have proved as ingenious at fabricating new threats (such as nuclear wastes) as at dealing with old ones. Nevertheless, we have reason to be hopeful, if not optimistic, that we can handle noxious accompaniments without necessarily eliminating the desired goods and services they attend. Perhaps we can learn to do the same with red tape.

Unfortunately, red tape is *not* the same as unwanted material by-products. The latter are easily distinguished from the desired products with which they are associated, and people by and large agree on what is product and what is waste no matter how bitterly they may quarrel over the acceptable balance between the two. In the case of government requirements and restraints, both substantive and procedural, people disagree about what is valued output and what is dismal by-product. As I observed at the very beginning of this book, what one interest calls deplorable another describes as precious; one person's red tape is another's sacred protection. Reducing "noxious" elements is infinitely harder under these conditions than containing the wastes of industry, difficult as that is. Successful general remedies are therefore hard to contrive.

THE FRUITLESS QUEST FOR
GENERAL REMEDIES

Intractable problems often engender proposals for sweeping solutions. In the case of red tape, the sweeping proposals are of four kinds. The first two attribute red tape primarily to the size of the federal government and recommend drastic reductions in federal activities, either by simple withdrawal of many kinds of services and cessation of many forms of regulation or by a transfer of functions to state and local governments, which are at least smaller than their federal counterpart and are said by some of their champions to be "closer to the people." The third ascribes red tape largely to the autonomy of departments and bureaus in the executive branch and urges stronger central controls as a way of offsetting the chaos and confusion produced by the multitude of free-wheeling units. The fourth attempts to avoid the extremes by using government authority in a new way—to provide incentives to private interests to do what the government wants instead of employing regulation or government operation for this end.

The advocates of each strategy seem absolutely assured that their favored plan will virtually do away with red tape. To the unconverted, however, these grand promises seem grossly overdrawn.

Shrinking the Government

Distrust of the federal government has a long history in this country. From the very start of the republic, many people were suspicious of our central institutions, regarding them as necessary evils to be kept to a minimum in size and scope. The tradition has never died.

Of course, the social groupings opposing and backing the central government have switched positions in the course of the years. The Jeffersonians, for example, spoke for middle- and lower-income groups in their hostility toward the federal government, while the Hamiltonian defenders of the federal government were allied with the more affluent commercial and industrial interests. Later, the less fortunate members of society allied themselves with vigorous, expansionist federal leaders, and the business community cried out for containment of our central organs of government. Attitudes seem to follow the flow of benefits.

Consequently, there has never been a time when advocates of minimal government have been without support among influential groups. They could not stop the steady enlargement of federal size and scope; the causes of growth have consistently overwhelmed them. But as the volume and variety of constraints reach a level at which they touch nearly everybody, subjecting more and more people to "pointless" requirements and miring more and more people in the quicksands of official procedures, the argument in favor of shrinking the government may well appeal to an ever larger and more sympathetic audience.

The essence of the argument is that the burdens and costs of red tape entailed in federal regulation and service are real and heavy while the alleged benefits are mostly illusory. Take rent control, for example. Supposed to serve the interests of tenants, it is said to make investment in rental properties so unattractive that the supply of housing does not keep pace with the demand for it. As a result, competition for an inadequate number of rental units keeps rents up even though the housing stock grows older and more outdated. Furthermore, rental-property owners, seeking to preserve a reasonable return on investments, tend to reduce expenditures on maintenance, so the condition of rental units deteriorates although rents remain at legal ceilings. If enforcement of building codes is intensified in an effort to force owners to increase maintenance, many structures are simply abandoned. Things grow worse and worse for tenants.

In contrast, it is said, if there were no rent control, rising rents and the prospects of good profits would induce many investors to erect new buildings. The increase in housing supply would check the upward spiral of rents as demand was met, older properties would be rehabilitated to make them competitive, and the charges for less desirable and older units would fall because they would fail to attract tenants unless they offered a significant price advantage. Thus, in the long run, tenants would presumably be better off without government protection. Parallel arguments have also been made for many other areas of regulation; the supposed advantages for consumers are described as momentary and minimal, the costs as extended, heavy, and cumulative. If the government abandoned regulation, we would all get more of what we want and need, and at the same time the volume of red tape with which we all have to put up would be dramatically reduced. Everyone—tenants, landlords, and builders —would allegedly be better off.

Corresponding logic applies to government services. Subsidies help keep alive economic units that would ordinarily be wiped out by market forces—such units are typically less efficient than the ones that can withstand competition. It therefore follows that the consumers of what these units produce bear a double burden—higher prices because of the inefficiencies, higher taxes because of the subsidies. In the case of assistance to the poor, it is alleged that many people prefer doing nothing if they get subsistence support to working full-time for wages not much higher. Wage scales are thus driven up to attract workers, so the cost of living is elevated. This raises the amount required for subsistence, so tax revenues must be increased to maintain the real level of public assistance. The economy is hampered by paid idleness and high taxes—and all the red tape both cause. Were the government to cut down the amount of support and the number of people supported—not to zero, of course, for even the most devout believer in the wisdom of the marketplace would temper its impersonality with compassion, but to levels much lower than many well-meaning people recommend and even than currently obtain—the efficiency of the economy would improve and all the people would enjoy more of the things they seek while simultaneously attaining greater freedom from the curse of red tape.

These contentions have great force as well as appeal for anyone weary of the way things have been tending in recent times. They may even triumph over prevailing tendencies some day. But the prospects of such a victory are not bright despite the attractiveness of the logic. Powerful contrary factors militate against comprehensive governmental shrinkage.

Chief among these is the danger that many of the evils and follies, both intentional and unwitting, against which the constraints scored as red tape are directed, might resurge if the measures taken to suppress them were lifted. More people might be harmed by the marketing of contaminated food, adulterated milk, or falsely labeled items. More investors would be fleeced by financial manipulators and unscrupulous stock speculators. Many professions, careers, and institutions once totally closed to members of ethnic minorities and to women would reclose without leaving a crack. The despoliation of the environment would be much worse without governmental safeguards, however deficient, and the outlook for the future much more depressing. The plight of the poor without at least minimal assistance would be desperate, and public order would be shaky if even more people were despairing than are now. The corruption and domination of government by those with money would become flagrant and arrogant and widespread. Clients would be helpless before the power of administrative agencies. Poverty-stricken tenants would be out in the streets before the market provided them with even inadequate shelter.

Admittedly, some of the governmental efforts to prevent such things have not been highly effective, some have exacerbated conditions they were meant to improve, and some have even produced side effects as painful as the social ailments they were supposed to cure. In such cases, only the direct beneficiaries would oppose elimination. Still, knowing how people behaved before the constraints were imposed inclines one to reject blanket proposals to drop the constraints *wholesale*. The remedies may work imperfectly, but things could be so much worse without them that even with their deficiencies and costs most of them cannot be lightly discarded.

Another factor counteracting the case for shrinking the government is the substantial sunk cost in ongoing federal programs and services. When a program or service is instituted, people adjust to it, and their calculations include its operations in their assumptions and reasoning. Producers in regulated industries, for example, take it for granted that their competitors, in the main, have to observe the same requirements that they do, and their decisions about investment, production, marketing, pricing, and other activities vital to the survival of their businesses are made in the light of these contraints. Removal of the constraints would not only subject them to great uncertainties, but might ruin them because many business and personal obligations, sound when undertaken on the basis of the rules then in force, must be honored even though the regulations have been drastically changed. Some producers, of course, would be favored by such changes in the business environment and would welcome them. Debarred but aspiring entrants into previously regulated fields would also applaud the removal of entry barriers by deregulation. But many established firms, having acted in good faith according to standards prescribed by government, would be hard hit and would naturally feel they had been misled. And many neutral observers would have to agree with them.

Similarly, the direct beneficiaries of subsidies, assistance, insurance, guarantees, loans at less than market interest, and other government benefactions would find their lives and livelihoods overturned by a sudden withdrawal of these supports. And consumers of products and services regulated by government also come to rely on these protections for their safety and welfare; termination of public protections would compel many of them to change their habits and allocations of resources in order to adjust to the new situation, and they would still feel anxious and unhappy about the responsibilities thrust back upon them. Large components of life patterns formed under a government shield against certain risks would be uprooted.

Perhaps people ought to be more flexible. Perhaps products and services would be improved by the goad of implacable competition. Perhaps the transition from present practices to dramatically reduced government could be accomplished in a gradual, nontraumatic fashion, easing the problems of accommodation. Nevertheless, there is no denying that reducing public services would be far from costless. Though government activities bring red tape in their wake without always yielding the advantages claimed for them, it is equally true that doing away with them would mean pain and distress for many besides the bureaucrats who would be displaced in a massive contraction. The balance sheet contains debits as well as credits.

Thus, on its merits and demerits alone, shrinking the government would encounter heavy sledding. And the diversity of interests in America would add to resistance against it. Even if everybody agreed in principle that terminating government programs was the best way to reduce red tape, experience indicates that each interest group construes this blanket policy to include only the programs that it cares little or nothing about, not the programs from which it benefits directly. Remote activities are expendable; those that hit close to home are indispensable. In these circumstances, the inevitable outcome is logrolling. Groups join in the defense of things to which they are indifferent in order to win allies for the things they are really concerned about. In the end, practically nothing will disappear. The sweeping rollback will break up on the endless variety in the system.

Simultaneously, the causes of governmental growth will continue with full force; powerful tendencies in this direction assert themselves constantly despite the complaints about government mismanagement and red tape. In the first few months of 1976, for example, a number of agencies came under fire for not using their authority vigorously enough rather than for excessive regulation. The Food and Drug Administration was attacked for being too permissive about the introduction of new drugs.[1] The Federal Home Loan Bank Board, the Federal Reserve System, and the Comptroller of the Currency were sued by a coalition of civil rights and housing groups for failing to prevent discrimination against racial and ethnic minorities and others by lending institutions.[2] The Equal Employment Opportunity Commission was castigated editorially for alleged inadequacies in enforcing statutory prohibitions against bias in hiring.[3] Three nuclear engineers charged the Nuclear Regulatory Commission with inadequate protection of the public against the hazards of nuclear-powered generation of electricity.[4] The Department of Health, Education, and Welfare was scored for failing to request sufficient funds and staff to deter widespread fraud in Medicaid.[5] The General Accounting Office criticized the Treasury Department for not seeking enough enforcement officers to assure compliance with the civil rights requirements by the recipients of revenue sharing money.[6]

1. James S. Turner, *The Chemical Feast* (Grossman, 1970), chaps. 10 and 11; *Use of Advisory Committees by the Food and Drug Administration*, H. Rept. 94-787, 94:2 (GPO, 1976), pp. 4, 5–6, 8, 9.

2. Ernest Holsendolph, *New York Times*, April 27, 1976. See also Austin Scott, *Washington Post*, June 1, 1976, for a finding by the Senate Banking Committee that there was strong evidence to justify the suit.

3. Editorial, *Washington Post*, April 28, 1976. See also the rejoinder of Daniel E. Leach, a member of the EEOC, in ibid., May 8, 1976, which puts the blame for deficiencies on inadequate budgets and insufficient staff.

4. David Burnham, *New York Times*, February 19, 1976.

5. Nancy Hicks, ibid.

6. Editorial, *Washington Post*, October 19, 1975; Warren Brown, ibid., June 3, 1976.

President Ford sought to expand the presidential staff within a year after taking office despite the disquiet about "the imperial presidency" following the Watergate revelations.[7] A subcommittee of the Senate Committee on Government Operations recommended federal regulation of independent auditors (accounting firms) that are now self-regulating.[8] Many people want more constraints, not fewer.

Indeed, despite the uproar over the excessive size and complexity of government, new units of organization, new programs, and new activities appear constantly.[9] In 1976, for example, neither the preoccupation of politicians with hard-fought battles over the nomination and election of the President nor the public commitment of both major candidates to restraining governmental growth prevented the enactment of statutes establishing at least five new administrative bodies in the executive branch,[10] not to mention those set up by departmental orders or other lesser instruments of creation. The thrust toward governmental growth seems almost irrepressible.

More government, not less, also comes from the search for coordination, which leads to "layering"—the insertion of additional administrative levels into existing structure. The classic illustration is the Department of Defense, which encompassed the old War and Navy Departments as well as the new Department of the Air Force, all of which continued at

7. David E. Rosenbaum, *New York Times,* July 10, 1975.
8. John F. Berry, *Washington Post,* January 17, 1977.
9. See Herbert Kaufman, *Are Government Organizations Immortal?* (Brookings Institution, 1976).
10. The U.S. Parole Commission (in the Department of Justice), 90 Stat. 219; the Office of Science and Technology Policy (in the Executive Office of the President; the act also created the President's Committee on Science and Technology and the Federal Coordinating Council for Science, Engineering, and Technology), 90 Stat. 459; the Commission on Security and Cooperation in Europe, 90 Stat. 661; the Office of Energy Information and Analysis (in the Federal Energy Administration), 90 Stat. 1135; and the Federal Grain Inspection Service (in the Department of Agriculture), 90 Stat. 2868-9.

the subcabinet level.[11] But the process takes place within departments, too; the National Oceanic and Atmospheric Administration, for instance, was a new echelon created between the Secretary of Commerce and several bureaus of the department.[12] In each case, an organization was established to pull together, in some sense, the work of existing agencies; the strategy also increased the total number of agencies, the sources of rules and regulations, and the multiplicity of vetoes and reviews to which administrative actions are subject. So has the creation of interagency coordinating committees, which abound in the executive branch.

The logic of rolling back the scope and intensity of government activities thus contends with the hard realities of strong countervailing trends. Commitment to the argument and the struggle to make it prevail are not necessarily in vain; after all, who knows where the countervailing trends might carry us if there were no determined opposition to them? All the same, in the near future, a sizable reversal of the deep-rooted tendencies toward continued growth does not seem likely.

But if by some miracle a large-scale reversal *did* suddenly come about, it is reasonable to anticipate that it would soon be followed and nullified by a resurgence of governmental growth. The factors that brought about the present situation

11. The origins of the Department of Defense are in the National Security Act of 1947, 61 Stat. 495; it became an executive department in 1949, 63 Stat. 578; see *1974/75 United States Government Manual,* p. 150. See also President Nixon's proposal for the creation of four new superdepartments in *Papers Relating to the President's Departmental Reorganization Program* (GPO, revised February 1972).

12. Reorganization Plan No. 4 of 1970, 84 Stat. 2090. Actually, NOAA replaced a previously established intermediate echelon, the Environmental Science Services Administration (Reorganization Plan No. 2 of 1965, 79 Stat. 1318), which nominally was a consolidation of the old Weather Bureau and Coast and Geodetic Survey; a number of fisheries functions and agencies from the Department of the Interior and some functions of the Defense Department were added when NOAA was formed. But the principal old bureaus, though modified, still survive as the major constituents of NOAA: the National Weather Service, the National Ocean Survey, and the National Marine Fisheries Service.

would create it again. The only way to prevent that would be to alter or eliminate those factors; wiping away their effects is only a temporary palliative if the causes that produced the effects endure. To modify those factors, sweeping changes in our society, our economy, and our political system might be necessary. Social orders are not immutable, of course; the people can grow frustrated enough to embark on a revolutionary course even though the outcome of such an adventure is uncertain. They would probably never revolt, however, merely because they were fed up with red tape. Red tape does not seem a sufficient provocation for such a radical set of actions, especially since there is no guarantee that a new order will be freer of red tape. So the causes of governmental growth will remain and the effects will reappear.

In these circumstances, only carefully selected, egregious, generally acknowledged failures among governmental activities stand a chance of elimination. Such modest measures would not significantly reduce the body of federal red tape. But they would doubtless accomplish more than attempts at an all-encompassing contraction of government on all fronts simultaneously.

Devolving Federal Power

This may be one reason why some who dream of severe, swift cuts in federal red tape suggest redistributing government functions and authority and responsibility instead of simply reducing them. The futility of striving for a rollback on all fronts evidently gives these critics pause. They therefore propose a different sort of remedy—transferring activities from the federal government to state and local governments.

This proposal seemingly proceeds from a different premise about the causes of the disagreeable features of government requirements and prohibitions than the proposal for a general contraction. The latter is apparently based on a belief in the inevitability of unpleasant consequences whenever public institutions undertake anything, especially when they engage in a wide variety of different programs. The devolution recommendation implies that the unpleasant consequences flow in large part from the concentration of activities in one level of government. The resulting congestion presumably causes the unhappy results we call red tape. Dispersing the activities is therefore the indicated way to alleviate the distress.

Of course, congestion is not the main reason for fearing concentration of power. Concentrated power is hard to resist and therefore drifts toward tyranny. The effects on red tape are minor by comparison.

But if these effects are overshadowed, they still are not negligible. Concentration can produce congestion because it leads to communications overloads. Channels may be clogged with messages to and from the field because agency headquarters must send elaborate instructions to field agents to guide their behavior in every outpost, and field personnel trying to make sure they comply with the directives find it necessary to request clearances, clarifications, directions for unanticipated cases, and other assistance or approvals. Headquarters offices thereupon swell to handle the burden. In the end the new units simply add to the traffic jam. Moreover, difficulties of coordination appear within headquarters as they expand, so new levels are created to overcome these deficiencies. The new levels, however, mean more steps in the communications process, slowing decisionmaking still further. It thus takes longer and longer to arrive at decisions, and when policies and judgments are finally settled, they are so remote from the people who must abide by them and enforce them that they frequently prove irrelevant to local conditions. They are therefore condemned as the foolish meddling of distant, presumptuous officialdom.

Hence, according to this school of thought, devolution is desirable not only for the major reason that it constitutes a bulwark against tyranny, but also because it incidentally reduces the conditions referred to as red tape. First, by bringing government decision centers closer to the people supposed to obey government decisions, devolution would increase the probability of local needs and conditions being recognized and taken into account. It would also afford local interests better opportunities to take part in the formation of policies directly affecting them. Not only would decisions then accord more closely with local circumstances; the decisions would also be more acceptable to the local populace because people are more inclined to tolerate actions in which they participate than actions from which they are excluded.[13] What would be considered red tape if centrally imposed might be regarded as reasonable constraint if arrived at locally.

Second, things would move faster if few matters had to be referred to the center before they could be resolved. The proverbial timidity of the bureaucrat and the collective evasiveness of bureaucracies would decline because the buck could be less easily passed to distant superiors. Communications channels would not be jammed with inquiries and requests flowing upward and commands and elaborations flowing down. So another source of irritation about government operations would be removed.

This reasoning is part of the underpinning of federal revenue sharing and grant consolidation that are now official policy. General revenue sharing is a block grant made according to a formula to all subnational units of general government in the country; it supplements a multitude of "categorical" grants for fairly specific purposes, for which recipients have to apply and which entail substantial restrictions on the discretion of all agencies that accept such awards. "Block grants" is the term used to describe grants for individual functions, such as community development, that con-

13. See the section on "Participation in Decision Making," in Victor H. Vroom, "Industrial Social Psychology," in Gardner Lindzey and Elliot Aronson, *The Handbook of Social Psychology*, 2d ed. (Addison-Wesley, 1969), vol. 5, pp. 227–39.

solidate a number of previously narrow categorical programs into a single broader one, replacing several separate applications by eligible governments with only one and relaxing some constraints on the recipients. Both forms of assistance retract federal control over state and local governments without cutting off the supply of federal funds. At the same time, inside the executive branch of the federal government, devolution of authority has been advanced by internal deconcentration through such means as establishment of common regional boundaries by various departments, adoption of common cities for their regional headquarters, and formation of councils or boards of regional officials and other field officers.[14]

Whether these strategies will significantly diminish the complaints about federal red tape is still in the realm of conjecture. Experiments so far are too recent and perhaps too limited to furnish probative answers. Deductively, however, some costs of devolution suggest themselves, and these indicate that devolution, like shrinking the role of government in society, has powerful factors working against it as well as for it.

First among these is the dissipation of national policies when constraints on lesser jurisdictions or subordinate administrators are lifted. Take, for example, the area of civil rights and liberties. Officers and employees of state and local governments, private firms and individuals, and even field employees of federal agencies in some parts of the country once engaged routinely in practices that conflicted with what the courts were eventually to recognize as constitutional guarantees; abuses of power are not exclusively, or even chiefly, federal. Through years of patient and sometimes heartbreaking toil, the aggrieved groups secured rulings from the federal courts, statutes from Congress, orders from various presidents,

14. Appendix D, *United States Government Manual*. (The first map of the Standard Federal Regions appears in the issue for 1972–73, p. 604. Descriptions of the regions, councils, and boards, as well as a map, have appeared in every issue since then.)

and administrative action from relevant federal agencies implementing those protections of the Constitution against infringement by these and other offenders. Although there is clearly a long way to go before the promise of the Constitution for all residents of the country is fully realized, such progress as has been made must be attributed in large measure to the interventions of the federal government on the side of the aggrieved. Obviously, those who have achieved hard-won victories in Washington will not passively acquiesce in the transfer of authority to jurisdictions where these groups have had a history of defeat and neglect. Recent moves by the federal government to recover a grant from a community allegedly violating federal civil rights provisions may reduce such fears, but civil rights activists will remain skeptical until it is demonstrated that this policy is both serious and effective.

Or take grants-in-aid by the federal government to states and localities given not simply to finance activities at those levels, but as inducements to those units of government to serve federal objectives by undertaking, increasing, or improving specified programs. Theoretically, if the leaders of the federal government were dissatisfied with the way state and local institutions were handling, or failing to handle, these functions, they could set up federal agencies to perform them directly. In practice, political and administrative obstacles obliged them to act through state and local institutions to deal with certain matters of national concern. The conditional grant-in-aid, contingent on fulfillment of federally stipulated terms by the recipients, was devised for this purpose; in a sense, it is a "bribe" to induce the recipients to do what federal officers want done. Nominally, state and local officials could decline the aid rather than submit to the strings attached to it and the resulting narrowing of their autonomy, but their financial condition does not afford most of them the luxury of such independence, especially since the money for the grants comes out of general federal tax revenues to which their own residents have contributed. The device has worked so well that highly specialized grant programs have proliferated. The federal government has succeeded in getting others to do what it could not win assent to do itself.

Those who wish to promote specific public activities are therefore uneasy about the possible consequences of devolution because they believe the results obtained through grants-in-aid would be jeopardized if the financial incentive to maintain them were removed—if funds were given free of all conditions about how they were to be used.[15] Certainly, people trying to encourage *new* policies that the federal government itself cannot execute will see no hope of winning their points without attaching strings to grants; free money, they contend, will go only for old functions. In other words, despite the red tape associated with categorical forms of assistance, it would not be easy to eliminate them or, if they were eliminated, to prevent them from reappearing in connection with new programs.

Quite apart from protective attitudes toward specific programs, general concern for uniform application of policy also militates against wholesale devolution. Not that uniformity

15. See, for example, the testimony of Gary Orfield in *State and Local Fiscal Assistance Act,* Hearings before the Intergovernmental Relations and Human Resources Subcommittee of the House Committee on Government Operations, 94:1 (GPO, 1975), pt. 2, pp. 1214–19. Note also the preference of the representative of retired persons, John M. Martin, for earmarking funds for the poor and the elderly, in ibid., p. 925.

Another such argument was advanced by Stephen K. Bailey and Edith K. Mosher, *ESEA: The Office of Education Administers a Law* (Syracuse University Press, 1968), pp. 214–15. Discussing whether federal aid to education should be granted unconditionally or with strings attached, they came out strongly in favor of attaching conditions to educational grants. "To argue," they said, "that all Federal money for education should be allocated to the States and localities with no strings attached whatsoever, is to argue that the national educational interest is identical with State and local interpretations of educational necessity. And it assumes that State and local educational agencies, unaided, have the staff, the talent pool, the imagination, and the freedom from irrational local pressures to use substantial increases in resources with creative wisdom in the national interest. Nothing in our past and present experiences as a nation suggests that any of these postulates is valid."

automatically assures equity or equality of treatment. Indeed, there is much to be said for diversity because it permits adjustment to special circumstances and it facilitates experimentation. In such cases, it is often adopted and it often succeeds. But if people in one region discover that they are treated differently from people in other regions under the same program, they are apt to be resentful and uncooperative. Moreover, some policies are unlikely to be effective unless they are managed on a national basis; energy conservation, pollution control, transportation development, and economic planning, for instance, can hardly be effective if they are not broadly conceived and executed. Consequently, vast areas of federal activity cannot be devolved despite the red tape they entail.

In any event, people whose demands on government are not met at the state and local levels or at lower levels of the federal hierarchy will not hesitate to try their luck in Washington. Our political system was constructed to provide numerous points of access; it is entirely appropriate to take advantage of these opportunities. But this means that every effort will be made at the federal level to reverse unfavorable actions by subnational authorities or parochial majorities. The federal government is an instrument of redress for those thwarted elsewhere. As a result, there is always as much thrust toward the center as away from it.

Centripetal tendencies might be less powerful if the federal government had fewer resources, if the world were a less hazardous place for a rich and democratic nation, if the industrial system did not make for such interdependence among all the components of our society, or if human rights and equality of treatment were not matters of national concern. Since these are the circumstances to which we must accommodate, however, the federal government will find itself unable to divest itself of responsibility for what happens below. More forces pull duties to it than push them away.

Concentrating Authority

The greater the dispersal of functions and the diffusion of authority in the governmental process, the stronger are the centripetal tendencies. Fragmentation itself breeds the very things decried as red tape.

In a highly decentralized governmental process, a profusion of authoritative organs can produce myriad inconsistent constraints, duplicative procedures, and vetoes. Numerous small units mean many boundaries, and every move across jurisdictional lines can mean new procedures to master, new permissions to obtain, new applications to file, new requirements and prohibitions to learn. For enterprises of greater than local scope, a decentralized system can mean having to comply with a wide variety of unrelated ordinances, statutes, rules, regulations, and decisions, many of them difficult to reconcile if not hopelessly incompatible. Decentralization can also subject communities to injury from neighbors acting in their parochial interests, as when upstream communities contaminate the drinking water and recreational facilities of those downstream[16] or when confusion and competition among state, county, and city officials in an area racked by conflict over school busing result in more severe rioting, according to neutral observers, than would have occurred had there been some overarching institution to bring them together.[17] Furthermore, some economies and efficiencies of scale are forgone when decentralization is chosen.

Many critics of red tape therefore recommend concentrating power. Centralized organs, they say, can "cut through"

16. The problem of external diseconomies—and economies—is not a simple one; "External Economies and Diseconomies," *International Encyclopedia of the Social Sciences* (Macmillan and Free Press, 1968). Whether or not the marketplace can make adjustments for some commercial costs and benefits, however, there is not much doubt that the burdens of externalities imposed by one public jurisdiction on others often remain unresolved and festering unless adjudicated by some higher authority—which runs counter to decentralization.

17. Paul Delaney, *New York Times,* June 16, 1976.

tangles and impose rationality and efficiency on a "crazy quilt" of discrete elements. That is why the government set up an Office of War Mobilization to direct the war effort in World War II and assigned to it responsibility for directing the country's reconversion to a peacetime footing when the war ended.[18] That is why a Housing Expediter was established at the end of the war to handle the housing market pressure generated by the release of postwar demand after five years of minimal construction.[19] That is why direction of the war on poverty in the 1960s was entrusted to the Office of Economic Opportunity, a command post in the Executive Office of the President, rather than to the profusion of existing agencies in the federal government and the states.[20] That is why the government turned to an energy "czar" to handle the fuel emergency of 1973 and its aftermath,[21] and why environmentalists sought to have one highly placed agency with broad powers manage the campaign for air and water purity.[22] That is one of the reasons one hears occasional calls for

18. Herman M. Somers, *Presidential Agency* (Harvard University Press, 1950), especially chap. 7: "The Continuing Need for Program Coordination."

19. Richard O. Davies, *Housing Reform during the Truman Administration* (University of Missouri Press, 1966), pp. 40–51, especially pp. 43–44.

20. Sar A. Levitan, *The Design of Federal Antipoverty Strategy* (Institute of Labor and Industrial Relations, University of Michigan and Wayne State University, 1967), pp. 26–30; and Adam Yarmolinsky, "The Beginnings of OEO," in James L. Sundquist, ed., *On Fighting Poverty* (Basic Books, 1969), p. 47.

21. The Federal Energy Administration was not the final word in the attempt to coordinate the effort to conserve and develop energy, however. The search for an organization to exercise leadership over some twenty-five agencies involved directly with fuel or energy problems was to continue for years; see *Energy Policy and Resource Management,* prepared by the Congressional Research Service for the Subcommittee on Energy of the House Committee on Government Operations, 93:2 (GPO, 1974), pp. 3–10; and *Federal Energy Reorganization,* a report to the Senate Committee on Government Operations prepared by the Congressional Research Service for Senator Charles H. Percy, 94:2 (GPO, 1976), pt. 2.

22. The Council on Environmental Quality was established in 1969 (83 Stat. 852) to recommend environmental policies, and the Environmental Protection Agency was established in 1970 (Reorganization Plan No. 3, 84 Stat. 2086) to bring together in one agency a number of scattered

"federalizing" certain activities and services.[23] And that is why the battle against one form of red tape—federal paperwork—has been put under a single center in the government from time to time.[24]

The strategy seems to work to some extent, for a time. Seldom for very long, however. Whatever its merits on other grounds, its effect on red tape is slight. The unpleasant symptoms gradually reappear. The misgivings of the government minimalists and the decentralists about the consequences of congestion at the center are apparently not without foundation.

The fight against paperwork is a good example. It goes back a long way; one congressional committee traced it as far as 1810. But the pace of the struggle advanced sharply during the New Deal and the Second World War. Since 1938, one committee of Congress after another, two Hoover Commissions, several bodies in the executive branch, and the Commission on Federal Paperwork have turned their attention to the problem. One early product of these inquiries was the Federal Reports Act of 1942, intended to reduce the federal paperwork load on businessmen.[25] It gave to the Bureau of

programs dealing with the environment. But environmental administration remained dispersed; Arnold W. Reitze, Jr., *Environmental Law*, 2d ed. (Washington: North American International, 1972), pp. 78–98. The search for a comprehensive instrumentality therefore continued; see, for example, *Congress and the Nation's Environment*, prepared by the Congressional Research Service for the Senate Committee on Interior and Insular Affairs, 93:1 (GPO, 1973), chap. 20.

23. In the welfare field, for instance, "complete federalization of categorical assistance costs has been urged by former HEW Secretary Wilbur Cohen, and on the Republican side by . . . Vice President Spiro Agnew"; Gilbert Y. Steiner, *The State of Welfare* (Brookings Institution, 1971), p. 20. Shifting financial burdens rather than reducing red tape was clearly the main purpose of these proposals, but red tape was doubtless a significant factor underlying them; see the testimony of John G. Veneman, Undersecretary of Health, Education, and Welfare, in *Problems in Administration of Public Welfare Programs*, Hearings before the Subcommittee on Fiscal Policy of the Joint Economic Committee, 92:1 (GPO, 1972), pt. 1, pp. 67–69.

24. See below, pp. 81–82, 82–89. See also *Congressional Quarterly Weekly*, vol. 33 (October 11, 1975), pp. 2168–69.

25. 56 Stat. 1078; see also Executive Order 10253, June 11, 1951.

the Budget "authority to order a single Federal agency to collect statistics if more than one is doing so, to determine whether or not the collection of data is necessary, to require an agency to make its statistics available to other agencies under certain conditions, and to approve or disapprove new plans to collect data from 10 or more persons." The bureau did its work so diligently that it was commended by a Senate committee in 1945 for "relieving business concerns of unnecessary reporting."[26]

Yet within a decade the whole system was under fire.[27] In part, it simply could not suppress the rising demand for information and revenue, which overwhelmed its initial successes. One may surmise that it also created new red tape inside the executive branch. All the agencies that once went directly to the public when they needed information now had new hurdles to clear—new clearances, new negotiations, new accommodations of other officials, new permissions to obtain —and at the same time were subjected to more demands for data by other agencies. What they once did quickly and simply had become an interagency process. Businessmen were spared; bureaucrats were burdened. The businessmen were to feel the effects, however, for the new procedures helped slow the process of governmental decisionmaking and action. The old complaints were heard again. In similiar fashion, the czars and expediters often add to the overall congestion in the system even if their initial effect is to break specific bottlenecks.

Sometimes, on the other hand, it is the long-range effects of centralization that are beneficial while the initial impact intensifies red tape. When the fourteen-member Commission on Federal Paperwork began its work in 1975, it found that, despite its numerous predecessors, it had to develop its own

26. *The Federal Paperwork Jungle,* H. Rept. 52, 89:1 (GPO, 1965), pp. 8–10.
27. *The Federal Paperwork Burden,* S. Rept. 93-125, 93:1 (GPO, 1973), p. 16; *Congressional Quarterly Weekly* (October 11, 1975), p. 2168.

information about prevailing practices in order to formulate sensible recommendations.[28] With a staff that reached a peak of 175 and a two-year budget exceeding $10 million, the commission produced a great deal of paper of its own and added temporarily to the work of some other federal agencies. Eventually, its ironic original situation notwithstanding, its labors will doubtless bring about substantial paperwork reductions and savings in selected areas. Initially, though, as it went about its business, the gross volume of paper inside the government increased rather than diminished. And since the commission probably will not slay the dragon of paperwork once and for all, other such bodies are likely to appear repeatedly; there will almost always be one trying to make things better in the future even if they have to make them worse in the present to achieve that goal.

Thus concentrating authority does not banish red tape any more than devolving power does. Sometimes it even adds to the problem.

Manipulating Pecuniary Incentives

The inadequacies of all three major approaches to the problem is one of the reasons for a proposal to attack it from a different angle, described by its author as "the public use of private interest."[29] Underlying this approach is a syllogism. It starts from the premise that the marketplace is a remarkable mechanism for the production and distribution of goods and services because it is driven by one of the most powerful forces in society: self-interest. But it is deficient because some values get little or no recognition in a system in which the pursuit of self-interest by all who take part in it is dominant. The government must therefore intervene.

28. *Congressional Quarterly Weekly* (October 11, 1975), pp. 2169–70. The personnel and budget figures presented later in the paragraph are from a member of the Paperwork Commission.

29. Charles L. Schultze, *The Public Use of Private Interest* (Brookings Institution, 1977).

Government intervention through the regulation of activities once left to the marketplace or through the direct provision of goods and services by government agencies brings with it its own alleged deficiencies, one of which is the proliferation of red tape. The new approach is to reach for the best of both the market and the governmental mechanisms, taking advantage of the powerful motivations of the former and the public-interest orientation of the latter. Instead of having the government tell people what to do and what not to do or having the government do things itself, the proposal is that taxation and subsidies be used to induce people to act, out of self-interest, in what the government considers the public interest. Many existing market incentives are the result of government policies, such as protection of patent rights, stabilization of money and credit, and tariffs. It would therefore be consistent with our traditions to employ public authority to provide further incentives when the existing incentive structure produces results the people find unsatisfactory.

The alleged beauty of this approach is that it skirts the shoals of red tape and inefficiency that government regulation and operation cannot avoid while attaining the social ends these policies are supposed to accomplish. It presumably combines the benefits of both the marketplace and government control without incurring the costs of either.

It is quite possible that the beneficial effects would be pronounced. There is certainly great promise in employing tax burdens and advantages and the granting or withholding of subsidies to influence behavior because these measures allow each individual and organization to invent compliant responses instead of being locked into prescribed ways of doing things. The spur of competition and the rewards of innovation are thus retained.

But it is far from obvious that this method would necessarily reduce red tape. The contention is persuasive only if one assumes that the collection and distribution of money by

83

the government entail less red tape than does regulation or
direct government operation and that government financial
powers are easier to administer, less burdensome, and more
acceptable to the public than regulatory powers or public
services. The assumptions are not self-evidently valid. Both
experience and logic call them into question.

Taxation has become the chief source of complaints about
government-imposed paperwork. The number, complexity,
and frequency of tax forms and reports evoke more outcries
than any other governmental demand.[30] As requirement is
added to requirement, refinement to refinement, distinction
to distinction, the vexations accumulate geometrically. Controversy attends almost every change, no matter how carefully
spelled out. Taxation has already become one of the major
sources of what people think of as red tape. The more purposes it is made to serve, the worse it is likely to get.

Similarly, the distribution of subsidies and other forms of
assistance is not a smooth-flowing, unanimously lauded, virtually automatic process. The procedures for applying for
grants, the methods of establishing eligibility, the disputes
over amounts, and the steps in appealing adverse decisions
engender a good deal of dissatisfaction, especially when back-
logs build up. The historical record does not support the contention that red tape can be significantly reduced by this
means.

Neither does logical deduction. There is no reason to expect a smaller output of government directives from tax and
subsidy programs than from regulatory or service programs.
It is no simple matter to define what is taxable and what is
not, what qualifies for aid and what does not, and what the
extent of liability or eligibility should be. For example, the
Secretary of the Treasury, after studying for fifteen months
a plan to tax fringe benefits, concluded that the issue was too
complicated to be solved by a broad regulation.[31] "Rather,"

30. See pp. 7–8, 56–58, above.
31. James L. Rowe, Jr., *Washington Post,* December 26, 1976.

he was quoted as saying, "the question of whether fringe benefits result in taxable compensation to employees should continue to depend, as it presently does, on the facts and circumstances that exist in individual situations." That means more special forms, more record-keeping, more data to be supplied to tax officers, more appeals, just to improve and equalize revenue collection. It does not take a vivid imagination to visualize the consequences of using taxation for purposes besides raising revenue. The multiplication of categories would itself necessitate a flood of instructions, which would be followed by more instructions as unanticipated ambiguities presented new problems. New products, methods, and services would spark requests for advisory opinions from taxpayers trying to determine whether it was possible for them to stay in business under the new requirements. Complaints about the length of time needed to get answers to such inquiries would increase, the number of appeals would rise, and the frequency of extended court battles would likewise go up. To enforce these complicated laws and regulations, a larger body of enforcement agents would have to be set up.

Complex systems of subsidies would entail corresponding consequences.

In the end, therefore, it is not clear that manipulating incentives to achieve public ends would be any freer of paperwork and other kinds of red tape than regulation and government operation are. It may have other justifications, but rolling back red tape is not likely to be one of its accomplishments.

No Panacea

What, then, is to be done? The surest way to get rid of the red tape associated with the federal government is to shrink the federal government itself, but the prospects of shrinking it to even its size in the early twentieth century are not bright; the disadvantages would be too great for too many people. Devolution likewise is not free of costs balancing many of its gains, and some of the frustrations of decentralization can match those caused by federal red tape. Concentration of authority, on the other hand, undeniably is often responsible for congestion at the center, layering of administrative levels, and long lines of communication; its disadvantages, too, are discouraging. And even the ingenious proposal for taking advantage of private incentives through taxes and subsidies would apparently result in just as much government paper and procedural complexity as the currently prevailing techniques of government intervention in social and economic relations.

To make things still more complicated, the quantity of red tape is not fixed; it is always growing. For red tape tends to beget more red tape. When the government enters upon a program of protecting people from one another or from their officials, or takes steps to assure the integrity of its own processes, or refines its system of taxation, its pronouncements inevitably entail ambiguities. The way ambiguities are resolved determines whether specific people or groups are entitled to particular benefits or subject to particular constraints. For that reason, the government, through all forms of law—statutes, regulations, judicial decisions, and executive orders—is constantly clarifying categories. But each clarification in turn leaves areas of uncertainty at the new definitional borders even as it clears up the old ones. So the growth of the corpus of provisions goes on and on.

The more extensive the corpus of provisions becomes, the more extensive the policing must be to ensure compliance. That alone means more red tape for the affected clients. More extensive policing requires more enforcement agents, which in turn mean intensified measures to deter abuses of power and trust. Ultimately the result is more internal and external red tape.

Curiously, as constraints on discretion both outside and inside the government accumulate, they sometimes reach a point where their effect is to broaden the very discretion they were supposed to contain. When there are multitudinous categories and definitions, shrewd operators can find somewhere in the stack justification for almost anything they want to do. Since these unanticipated uses of legal provisions are frequently perceived as "loopholes," the standard response in government is to promulgate provisions "plugging" the loopholes. But the additional categories and definitions sometimes provide new opportunities for evasion. So the growth feeds on itself.

That is not to say the termination, transfer, or concentration of specific governmental activities or the manipulation of pecuniary incentives are *never* followed by their intended effects. On the contrary, they may reduce red tape significantly in specific instances, at least for a time. But it does not follow that they will succeed everywhere if they are applied wholesale. Even if they did not clash with each other and even if there were not numerous sources of strong resistance to them, they would not be effective against many forms of red tape and they would frequently generate new kinds or foster its growth in new places. Their respective advocates sometimes give the impression that their favored formulas are remedies for red tape which, if taken in large doses, would reduce it to negligible proportions. For the reasons cited, such claims must be taken with a grain of salt. There is no panacea.

But there are ways of keeping red tape under control and endurable. They are not spectacular or glamorous. They work no miracles. Nevertheless, they can provide relief.

TREATING SYMPTOMS

Those ways are the normal methods of politics. The political system responds to pointed demands for specific actions, not to grand visions or all-embracing lamentations. Grand visions and ill-defined complaints, of course, often determine the particulars of demands. But until and unless they are translated into concrete measures that officials can act on, they seldom evoke any governmental response. They may win offers of sympathy, expressions of shared outrage, and even symbolic gestures of solidarity and support. But not tangible benefits.

Not that public officers and employees are arrogantly indifferent to nebulous petitions for action. Rather, such petitions give them either no clues to appropriate reactions or clues to conflicting and contradictory reactions. Since broad labels encompass hosts of incompatible wants and complaints, agitating for a cleaner environment or better health care or equal opportunity in general will produce pious endorsements for these sweeping goals though proposals for specified controls on pollutants, medical insurance, and affirmative action on behalf of minorities are what is needed to get the reform on the official agenda. Similarly, railing against all red tape or advancing some panacea that will purportedly dispose of it once and for all avails nothing; an attack on a particular procedure in a particular agency or on a designated tax or application form or on a specified requirement long since out of date is much more likely to get results.

That is why the federal government's paperwork demands on the public, especially on small businessmen, have received so much attention for the past generation. Critics concentrated on this set of irritants. Admittedly, it is a huge set, so huge that many critics equate red tape and paperwork. Actually, of course, there is much more to red tape than paperwork. But by focusing on this one part, big as it is, the critics were able to make some headway, engendering the Federal Reports Act and the aforementioned investigations of paperwork in both the legislative and executive branches.

Apparently the target was still too large, however. The discontent with paperwork persisted, leading to the Federal Paperwork Commission, whose assignment may be described as breaking the problem into still smaller, more manageable, concrete components and fashioning solutions for each.

This commission, unlike its predecessors, was neither confined to one branch of the government nor saddled with any responsibilities other than to "minimize the burden imposed by Federal reporting requirements on private citizens, recipients of Federal assistance, businesses, government contractors, and State and local governments."[32] It consisted of two members from each house of Congress, the Comptroller General, two representatives of the executive branch (the director of the Office of Management and Budget and the Commissioner of Internal Revenue), a governor, a county commissioner, and five public members. It commenced operations in 1975 and had up to two years to complete its task. Chances are federal paperwork never received so much undivided attention from such a high-level, well-financed, generously staffed body. The commission therefore had an opportunity to succeed where its predecessors did not.[33]

In all likelihood there would be no such commission were it not for the steady drumfire of complaint about paperwork maintained by small businessmen. They zeroed in on particular burdens, identifying as the main irritants the lengthy and numerous information reports they were obliged to fill out for the Social Security Administration, the Bureau of the Census, the Internal Revenue Service, and the Occupational Safety and Health Administration. They had specified targets. Their fire was focused.

Moreover, they made their views known through professional, articulate, politically sophisticated spokesmen. Taking up cudgels for them were such groups as the American Retail Association, the Financial Executives Institute, the National Federation of Independent Business, the National Retail Hardware Association, the Associated General Contractors of America, the Independent Broker-Dealers Trade Association, the National Society of Public Accountants, the

32. 88 Stat. 1789, §1.
33. But pessimism about its prospects were voiced even before its report was rendered; Paul H. Weaver, "That Crusade against Paperwork Is a Paper Tiger," *Fortune* (November 1976), pp. 118–21, 206–10.

Chamber of Commerce of the United States, and even the National Association of Manufacturers and the National Association of Broadcasters. Small wonder they were not ignored.

Of course, such an imposing array of petitioners is not necessary to obtain redress of every grievance. Generally, the narrower the complaint, the smaller the force that must be mobilized to get relief. But some mobilization is required for virtually all remedial action, and paperwork is a large enough subject to have necessitated an impressive show of strength and distress.

Nor is a top-level commission necessary to correct every instance of red tape. A change in specifications here, a relaxation of restrictions there, a restraining influence on an over-zealous agency, a prod for a sluggish one, an improvement in a single procedure, or a simplification of a single form may alleviate a great deal of pain for a great many people. An individual legislator or a member of his staff, the members or the staff of legislative or appropriations or budget committees or subcommittees, a journalist eager for a good story, a court, congenial bureaucrats, and competing agencies are among the points at which pressure can be quietly but effectively applied to induce a change. It is done all the time. A good many victories over red tape are won in this fashion.

Thus, although massive rollbacks of the provisions and procedures making up most of the red tape in government will not take place, neither will we inevitably be engulfed by a tidal wave of red tape. Through the normal processes of politics, the really exasperating irritants can and probably will be controlled. That may be disappointing to those who futilely wish for obliteration of the despised culprit. But those who remember how much relief can be brought by the removal of just a single grain of sand from the eye will take heart.

The traditional process of politics, however, will not do much for large numbers of persons lacking the knowledge,

the confidence, or the resources to exercise their theoretical rights. Even educated, experienced, relatively high-status citizens sometimes find themselves baffled or intimidated by government officers and employees. Occasionally, they calculate that the cost of fighting to get what they regard as legitimately theirs would exceed what they would get if they were successful. So they do not claim everything to which they may be entitled. Imagine, then, the predicament of those among us who do not enjoy the advantages of background and status. For them, Kafka's hair-raising nightmares are not flights of fancy; Kafka described the system that they encounter and recoil from, defeated, whenever they have business with it.

Admittedly, public bureaucracies in America are probably better in this regard than most foreign bureaucracies; ours are exceptionally open and vulnerable to exposure when their arrogance gets out of hand. Thanks to the mobilization of once unorganized interests—ethnic minorities, women, the poor, consumers, and others—things may well be better now than they ever were. Nevertheless, there are still a great many people who get less than they qualify for because the tangles of red tape in government put them off. If they can be helped as individuals to thread their way through these obstacles, the red tape would seem far less oppressive to them and to those concerned about their rights. Since the disease cannot be eliminated, it makes sense to help directly those it afflicts instead of channeling energy into a vain quest for a complete cure.

We have already taken a number of steps in this direction. The oldest, and among the most important, is the expansion of "case work" by the staffs of individual members of Congress.[34] As a legal obligation and also as a political necessity

34. Walter Gellhorn, *When Americans Complain* (Harvard University Press, 1966), pp. 57–73. See also the testimony of Congressman Gerald R. Ford, then minority leader of the House of Representatives, in *Committee Organization in the House*, Hearings before the House Select Committee on Committees, 93:1 (GPO, 1973), vol. 1, pt. 1, pp. 50–51; addressing the issue of constituency service, he noted, "I think it is a wholesome

for incumbents who wish to be reelected, "representation" has come to mean rendering aid to constituents in their contacts with bureaucracies as well as speaking for the constituents in the legislative process. A great many people routinely appeal to their legislators when they feel bewildered, helpless, or otherwise frustrated in their relations with the administrative organs of government, and some are significantly helped.

An unusual form of legislative assistance was employed by the junior United States senator from New Jersey in the spring of 1976.[35] Although the General Services Administration maintains Business Service Centers in major metropolitan areas to assist—indeed, to search out—businessmen seeking government contracts, the senator sponsored a one-day regional conference for economically hard-pressed businessmen in the northern part of the state for the purpose of instructing them on how to make their way through the rules and regulations governing the sale of goods and services to federal and state agencies. (The governor, the senior senator, and the representative from the district endorsed the conference.)

Some agencies themselves try to provide the public with comparable assistance and advice. One of the most familiar services of this kind is offered by the Internal Revenue Service, whose personnel are made available every year during income tax season to work with individual taxpayers who request help. Similarly, the district offices of the Social Security Administration and the contact officers of the Veterans' Administration serve as counselors and aides to those who call upon them. Field offices of other agencies also furnish this sort of support for the general public, but the scale and diversity of the clienteles of the IRS, the SSA, and the VA make

---

trend that we have added to our staffs. When . . . I came here, I recall we were permitted to have three, a very limited staff allowance. Today, we have 15 or 16." As a result, he added, many individual injustices and inequities have been corrected.

35. Walter H. Waggoner, *New York Times,* March 16, 1976.

their operations especially worthy of note. (Incidentally, although selfless generosity on the part of the agencies may account for some of this solicitude, the services are probably motivated to a much larger extent by organizational self-interest. They mollify citizens whose collective anger could be harmful to the organizations. They improve compliance with complicated legal requirements. And they reduce errors that would later entail more expense and difficulty for the organizations than are incurred in helping clients in the first instance. In this respect, the interests of the clients and the agencies coincide.)

More recently, the federal government, through its General Services Administration, introduced yet another device to assist the general public: Federal Information Centers.[36] Over three dozen major metropolitan areas have such facilities, and forty cities are connected to them by toll-free telephone lines. Their purpose is to "eliminate the maze of referrals which people too often have experienced" by functioning as clearinghouses for information about the federal government and often about state and local governments as well. "If a citizen has a question of any sort about the Government and has no idea which of the hundreds of offices can provide the answer, he may bring any such question to a Federal Information Center by phone, by visit, or by mail. The task of the FIC is to get the information you need or refer you to the expert who can." Many of these offices have personnel who speak foreign languages, and all of them offer government publications, including consumer information pamphlets. In fiscal year 1977, a decade after the first center opened, they handled 7.2 million inquiries as both the number of installations and the average number of calls at each location climbed swiftly.[37]

Some nongovernmental institutions do the same sorts of

36. *1976/77 United States Government Manual,* pp. XIII–XIV, 544. The quotations in the text are from p. 544.

37. Data furnished by the Coordinator of the Federal Information Centers Staff.

things with their own resources. The legal staffs of interest groups, such as veterans' organizations, trade unions, and ethnic associations, provide information and advice for individual members who ask for help and intercede as their representatives when necessary. Public-interest law firms and commercial law firms that customarily allocate some of their resources to public-interest work also take up the cudgels for the otherwise helpless. In the District of Columbia, a group of volunteers staffs a complaint center whose purpose is to advise callers about the way to get responses from the municipal government and to function as intermediary in some cases.[38] Some radio stations also undertake to help people in these ways—in relation not only to government but also to businesses with which they have had trouble.[39] (The problems of red tape, unfortunately, are not exclusively governmental.)

The appearance of all these bodies is evidence that through the normal processes of politics the government can be made to respond to the needs and desires of people frustrated by red tape. If traditional structures prove inadequate, new organizations come into existence to satisfy them.

Yet some students of government have concluded that even these organizations, in all their variety, are inadequate to relieve every person with a grievance against official action or inaction. Although the offices of legislators have been greatly enlarged over the years, population growth and the rising complexity of modern society have so expanded the demands on them that casework has become a pure formality in most instances—a routine transmittal of constituents' complaints to the relevant administrative agencies, routine reports to constituents on the agencies' replies. When agen-

38. Called the "City Hall Complaint Center," it is largely a telephone operation, but it is located in the building that houses the seat of government of the District of Columbia.

39. In Washington, D.C., for example, WTOP, using volunteers, operates the program "Call For Action" to assist frustrated members of the public.

cies furnish assistance to clients, the interests of the assisting officers are not unequivocally on the side of the clients; aggressive solicitude for clients' demands on the part of bureaucrats may clash with organizational loyalties and may damage career prospects if the solicitude causes complications that would not otherwise arise. Intercession by nongovernmental groups, though valuable, obtains relief for only a fraction of the people in need of aid because the resources of the public-interest organizations are limited and because so many people are not members of any interest groups at all. Information centers are likewise useful, but many people who need to deeply penetrate the thickets of official red tape require more assistance than these offices are equipped to provide.

Hence the interest in the ombudsman, the Swedish institution for pressing citizen complaints against government.[40] The Swedes introduced it in the nineteenth century, an addition to existing judicial and political and administrative remedies. It entered the discourse on public administration in this country only in the 1950s, when the permanence and political power of large public bureaucracies began to alarm those once imbued with New Deal enthusiasm for administrative growth. The general concept has won a great deal of support, and some jurisdictions have experimented with versions of it, but there is no consensus on details and no apparent likelihood of prompt adoption of the office at the federal level. Still, the persistence of the idea indicates that this additional possible tactic to help those who need special help in dealing with governmental red tape may yet give rise to some variety of it in the federal administrative establishment.

The ombudsman is, in essence, the head of a complaint bureau clothed with official power to receive and investigate complaints against administrative action anywhere in the administrative machinery of government. If the ombudsman

40. Gellhorn, *When Americans Complain;* Stanley V. Anderson, ed., *Ombudsman for American Government?* (Prentice-Hall, 1968); and Alan J. Wyner, ed., *Executive Ombudsmen in the United States* (Institute of Governmental Studies, University of California, Berkeley, 1973).

finds merit in a complaint, the expectation is that the accused agency will normally accede to his finding and redress the grievance as he recommends. If the agency does not, the ombudsman may appeal to higher administrative authority, to the courts, or even to the legislature for corrective action. The complainant, in short, would enjoy the services of a well-equipped champion whose resources would be comparable to those of other parts of the bureaucracy, a champion whose performance was measured by triumphs over bureaucratic adversaries. Incentives and power would run together to equalize battles between individual citizens and public agencies.

This reform will run into obstacles because it creates anxiety among legislators and administrative agencies already on the scene. Legislators tend to guard their functions fiercely, for the power of legislative bodies can be eroded by a series of seemingly small concessions; creating a rival for casework services to their constituents would be a very substantial concession, and their suspicion would not be easily put to rest. Administrative agencies wonder what the impact of an ombudsman on their operations would be, particularly since he could introduce impediments to crisp decisive action, and perhaps encourage resistance where none would otherwise develop. The division of responsibilities between an ombudsman and other investigative units, such as the General Accounting Office and the Department of Justice, is bound to lead to ambiguities that cause the latter some uneasiness.

Nevertheless, the gathering storm clouds of discontent with government in general signal some inadequacies in prevailing methods of helping people deal with red tape. Some equivalent of the ombudsman, added to the other mechanisms, might well reduce the frustrations. It is an avenue that will not be closed, at least to further experimentation.

Should it take firm hold eventually, however, it will by no means end red tape or the problems associated with red tape. Instead, it will add to the total corpus of red tape by introducing another agency making regulations and issuing judgments binding on others. Moreover, it is likely to get set in its ways and become the target of criticism indistinguishable from the charges leveled against other agencies. In Sweden, the institution is under attack for weakness and timidity.[41] In this country, the public defender, once hailed as a heroic improvement in the system of criminal justice, has not become the reforming instrument many of its advocates envisioned. In Cuba, an antibureaucratic unit was terminated in less than a year because, the premier announced with dry humor, it had become bogged down in red tape.[42] Institutional reforms are not immune to the viruses that infect large organizations generally. We may therefore anticipate that the procedures set up to ease the pains of red tape by assisting individuals trapped in the coils will themselves be denounced one day.

DEATH, TAXES, AND RED TAPE

Red tape has thus taken its place with death and taxes as an inevitability of life. It may even be more durable than they are. Heaven has no place for death and taxes, but it probably is not entirely free of red tape; after all, the rules in the Garden of Eden were pretty strict. At any rate, there is no escape from it on earth.

Maybe we could suppress it if it were merely the nefarious work of a small group of villains or if it were a waste product easily separated from the things we want of government, but it is neither. Anyway, if we did do away with it, we would be appalled by the resurgence of the evils and follies it currently prevents. Furthermore, despite our best efforts to eliminate it or even to reduce it, we seem to end up with more of it than

41. Bernard D. Nossiter, *Washington Post,* June 14, 1976.
42. The creation of the unit was reported in the *New York Times,* February 21, 1967; its demise was reported in ibid., May 24, 1967.

we had at the start. We are ambivalent about the appropriate trade-offs between discretion and constraint, each of us demanding the former for ourselves and the latter for our neighbors. Under these conditions, learning to live with it is the only thing to do.

Learning to live with it does not mean accepting all its manifestations and worst features, however. Rather, it means systematically laboring to maximize its net benefits while minimizing its net costs. What we need is a detached clinical approach rather than heated attacks, the delicate wielding of a scalpel rather than furious flailing about with a meat ax.

Dealing with bits and pieces of the problem will not yield dramatic results. Indeed, since there is little prospect of "breakthroughs," total solutions, or magic elixirs to banish it and since the world is growing more complex and interdependent all the time, an inexorable increase must be expected in the number of requirements and prohibitions with which we will have to put up. The best we can hope for is that the rate of growth will be sufficiently controlled to allow us to adjust to these additional irritants.

Even this limited goal will not be achieved easily. The volume of administrative regulations issued by the federal government has been increasing at a startling rate in recent years. In 1946, for example, the number of pages published in the *Federal Register* was just under 15,000. The annual total dropped to 10,528 in 1956, rose again to nearly 17,000 in 1966, and then soared to more than 57,000 in 1976. The Office of the Federal Register estimates that it will reach 100,000 pages a year in 1980.[43] This is a crude index; the pages include draft regulations (printed so that interested parties can comment on them) as well as final versions, and the wording of statutes is often repeated in regulations, so there is considerable duplication. Nevertheless, even allowing for duplication, the outpouring is dismaying. Containing the flood

43. Office of the Federal Register, *The Federal Register: What It Is and How to Use It* (GPO, 1977), p. 6.

of regulations and helping people deal with it will require determined, unremitting effort. Chipping away at a problem calls for more perseverance and stamina than blasting away at it.

From all indications, our descendants will be chipping away at it just as we are. For them, however, the character of the problem may be different. Automation, for instance, will contribute to change. Already, information from cash registers can be linked to accounting and inventory-control computers, reducing the flow of paper significantly. The day may come when hosts of other transactions are similarly recorded and transmitted automatically to vast data banks, where taxes and benefits and other obligations of people to governments, governments to people, governments to governments, and people to people are calculated by machine and added and subtracted from appropriate accounts with little human intervention. The present generation would probably view such a world with horror; the dangers of a whole social system manipulated through such centralized operations, the opportunities for sophisticated embezzlement and fraud, and the diminution of individual privacy are repellent to many of us. If paperwork continues to increase, however, future generations may regard the trade-off between higher risks and fewer nettling chores as well worthwhile. Values and practices will go on evolving, and with that evolution will come new definitions of red tape and new evaluations of unacceptable costs. The target never stops moving.

Even a fully wired and automated society would not be rid of red tape, though. Safeguards against abuses would be extensive. Methods of appeal from errors or abuses would have to be developed. Most of all, the machines themselves would impose an unyielding set of obligations and prohibitions on their users. Red tape of the future will undoubtedly be different in many respects from what we know today, but red tape there will certainly be.

The prospect is not a cheerful one. We can hardly look

forward with eager anticipation to continuous struggle against an enemy that will never be finally defeated yet may overwhelm us if our resolve flags. But is that not the human condition? Have not many of mankind's advances come from the confrontation of this harsh reality rather than from false optimism? Accepting red tape as an ineradicable foe is not to give up the fight, but to join battle on the only terms that offer any hope of success.

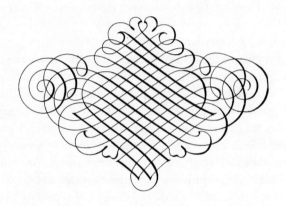